Dreamweaver® 4
FOR
DUMMIES®
QUICK REFERENCE

by Camille McCue

IDG
BOOKS
WORLDWIDE

IDG Books Worldwide, Inc.
An International Data Group Company

Foster City, CA ✦ Chicago, IL ✦ Indianapolis, IN ✦ New York, NY

Dreamweaver® 4 For Dummies® Quick Reference

Published by
IDG Books Worldwide, Inc.
An International Data Group Company
919 E. Hillsdale Blvd.
Suite 300
Foster City, CA 94404
www.idgbooks.com (IDG Books Worldwide Web site)
www.dummies.com (Dummies Press Web site)

Library of Congress Control Number: 00-111276

ISBN: 0-7645-0800-8

Printed in the United States of America

10 9 8 7 6 5 4 3 2 1

1O/RU/QS/QR/IN

Distributed in the United States by IDG Books Worldwide, Inc.

Distributed by CDG Books Canada Inc. for Canada; by Transworld Publishers Limited in the United Kingdom; by IDG Norge Books for Norway; by IDG Sweden Books for Sweden; by IDG Books Australia Publishing Corporation Pty. Ltd. for Australia and New Zealand; by TransQuest Publishers Pte Ltd. for Singapore, Malaysia, Thailand, Indonesia, and Hong Kong; by Gotop Information Inc. for Taiwan; by ICG Muse, Inc. for Japan; by Intersoft for South Africa; by Eyrolles for France; by International Thomson Publishing for Germany, Austria and Switzerland; by Distribuidora Cuspide for Argentina; by LR International for Brazil; by Galileo Libros for Chile; by Ediciones ZETA S.C.R. Ltda. for Peru; by WS Computer Publishing Corporation, Inc., for the Philippines; by Contemporanea de Ediciones for Venezuela; by Express Computer Distributors for the Caribbean and West Indies; by Micronesia Media Distributor, Inc. for Micronesia; by Chips Computadoras S.A. de C.V. for Mexico; by Editorial Norma de Panama S.A. for Panama; by American Bookshops for Finland.

For general information on IDG Books Worldwide's books in the U.S., please call our Consumer Customer Service department at 800-762-2974. For reseller information, including discounts and premium sales, please call our Reseller Customer Service department at 800-434-3422.

For information on where to purchase IDG Books Worldwide's books outside the U.S., please contact our International Sales department at 317-572-3993 or fax 317-572-4002.

For consumer information on foreign language translations, please contact our Customer Service department at 1-800-434-3422, fax 317-572-4002, or e-mail rights@idgbooks.com.

For information on licensing foreign or domestic rights, please phone +1-650-653-7098.

For sales inquiries and special prices for bulk quantities, please contact our Order Services department at 800-434-3422 or write to the address above.

For information on using IDG Books Worldwide's books in the classroom or for ordering examination copies, please contact our Educational Sales department at 800-434-2086 or fax 317-572-4005.

For press review copies, author interviews, or other publicity information, please contact our Public Relations department at 650-653-7000 or fax 650-653-7500.

For authorization to photocopy items for corporate, personal, or educational use, please contact Copyright Clearance Center, 222 Rosewood Drive, Danvers, MA 01923, or fax 978-750-4470.

is a registered trademark under exclusive license to IDG Books Worldwide, Inc., from International Data Group, Inc.

About the Author

Since 1988, **Camille McCue** has expended lots of sweat and only a few tears blending the fields of technology, television, and teaching. Her lighthearted approach to communicating science and computer content in print and on air has made her an award-winning educator, Web designer, author, and TV personality.

Camille currently works as a technology consultant and freelance television producer. She owns her own Web business — Cool Blue Design, LLC (www.coolbluedesign.com) — which provides clients with turnkey Web site solutions, from domain name registration to site design to hosting and promotion. When she's not clicking away online, Camille collaborates on instructional and community television projects for KLVX-TV, the PBS affiliate in Southern Nevada.

Not so long ago, Camille was a Texas gal, earning her B.A. in Mathematics from the University of Texas at Austin, and her M.A. in Education from the University of Texas at San Antonio. Following graduation, Camille went to work marketing PCs for IBM. She later became a tele-educator, instructing physics via satellite to rural kids nationwide, and then eventually creating live television events for NASA Headquarters in Washington, D.C. Most recently, Camille served as distance education faculty at UNLV and as Ready To Learn coordinator for KLVX-TV.

Since 1998, Camille has authored several technology titles for IDG Books Worldwide, Inc., including, *PowerPoint '97 For Windows For Dummies Quick Reference,* the *PowerPoint 2000* update, *CliffsNotes Finding What You Want on the Web,* and *CliffsNotes Exploring the Internet with Yahoo!.* Camille resides in Las Vegas (yes, people really do live there!) with her husband Michael — an Internet and intellectual property law partner with the firm of Quirk & Tratos — and their beautiful baby boy, Ian.

ABOUT IDG BOOKS WORLDWIDE

Welcome to the world of IDG Books Worldwide.

IDG Books Worldwide, Inc., is a subsidiary of International Data Group, the world's largest publisher of computer-related information and the leading global provider of information services on information technology. IDG was founded more than 30 years ago by Patrick J. McGovern and now employs more than 9,000 people worldwide. IDG publishes more than 290 computer publications in over 75 countries. More than 90 million people read one or more IDG publications each month.

Launched in 1990, IDG Books Worldwide is today the #1 publisher of best-selling computer books in the United States. We are proud to have received eight awards from the Computer Press Association in recognition of editorial excellence and three from Computer Currents' First Annual Readers' Choice Awards. Our best-selling ...For Dummies® series has more than 50 million copies in print with translations in 31 languages. IDG Books Worldwide, through a joint venture with IDG's Hi-Tech Beijing, became the first U.S. publisher to publish a computer book in the People's Republic of China. In record time, IDG Books Worldwide has become the first choice for millions of readers around the world who want to learn how to better manage their businesses.

Our mission is simple: Every one of our books is designed to bring extra value and skill-building instructions to the reader. Our books are written by experts who understand and care about our readers. The knowledge base of our editorial staff comes from years of experience in publishing, education, and journalism — experience we use to produce books to carry us into the new millennium. In short, we care about books, so we attract the best people. We devote special attention to details such as audience, interior design, use of icons, and illustrations. And because we use an efficient process of authoring, editing, and desktop publishing our books electronically, we can spend more time ensuring superior content and less time on the technicalities of making books.

You can count on our commitment to deliver high-quality books at competitive prices on topics you want to read about. At IDG Books Worldwide, we continue in the IDG tradition of delivering quality for more than 30 years. You'll find no better book on a subject than one from IDG Books Worldwide.

John Kilcullen
Chairman and CEO
IDG Books Worldwide, Inc.

Eighth Annual Computer Press Awards ≥1992

Ninth Annual Computer Press Awards ≥1993

Tenth Annual Computer Press Awards ≥1994

Eleventh Annual Computer Press Awards ≥1995

IDG is the world's leading IT media, research and exposition company. Founded in 1964, IDG had 1997 revenues of $2.05 billion and has more than 9,000 employees worldwide. IDG offers the widest range of media options that reach IT buyers in 75 countries representing 95% of worldwide IT spending. IDG's diverse product and services portfolio spans six key areas including print publishing, online publishing, expositions and conferences, market research, education and training, and global marketing services. More than 90 million people read one or more of IDG's 290 magazines and newspapers, including IDG's leading global brands — Computerworld, PC World, Network World, Macworld and the Channel World family of publications. IDG Books Worldwide is one of the fastest-growing computer book publishers in the world, with more than 700 titles in 36 languages. The "...For Dummies®" series alone has more than 50 million copies in print. IDG offers online users the largest network of technology-specific Web sites around the world through IDG.net (http://www.idg.net), which comprises more than 225 targeted Web sites in 55 countries worldwide. International Data Corporation (IDC) is the world's largest provider of information technology data, analysis and consulting, with research centers in over 41 countries and more than 400 research analysts worldwide. IDG World Expo is a leading producer of more than 168 globally branded conferences and expositions in 35 countries including E3 (Electronic Entertainment Expo), Macworld Expo, ComNet, Windows World Expo, ICE (Internet Commerce Expo), Agenda, DEMO, and Spotlight. IDG's training subsidiary, ExecuTrain, is the world's largest computer training company, with more than 230 locations worldwide and 785 training courses. IDG Marketing Services helps industry-leading IT companies build international brand recognition by developing global integrated marketing programs via IDG's print, online and exposition products worldwide. Further information about the company can be found at www.idg.com. 1/26/00

Dedication

To Ian.

Author's Acknowledgments

Thanks to the fantastic crew at IDG who perform such a great job of getting computer mumbo-jumbo turned into easy-to-use materials that I, too, buy at the bookstore! I'd like to convey special appreciation to Acquisitions Editor, Steve Hayes, who has made it possible for me to work on several exciting projects; and to Project Editor, Paul Levesque, who not only has a keen eye for assembling content, but can tell you to "speed it up" with the loveliest accent you've ever heard. Thanks also to Copy Editor, Beth Parlon, who has been kind enough to go through more than one of my books with a fine-tooth comb; and to Technical Editor Kyle Bowen, who checked every procedure step-by-step to ensure accuracy for our readers.

Publisher's Acknowledgments

We're proud of this book; please send us your comments through our IDG Books Worldwide Online Registration Form located at www.dummies.com.

Some of the people who helped bring this book to market include the following:

Acquisitions, Editorial, and Media Development

Project Editor: Paul Levesque

Acquisitions Editor: Steve Hayes

Copy Editor: Beth Parlon

Proof Editor: Seth Kerney

Technical Editor: Kyle Bowen

Permissions Editor: Carmen Krikorian

Editorial Manager: Leah Cameron

Editorial Assistant: Seth Kerney

Production

Project Coordinator: Leslie Alvarez

Layout and Graphics: Amy Adrian, Gabriele McCann, Jill Piscitelli, Kendra Span, Erin Zeltner

Proofreaders: Laura Albert, Linda Quigley, York Production Services, Inc.

Indexer: York Production Services, Inc.

General and Administrative

IDG Books Worldwide, Inc.: John Kilcullen, CEO; Bill Barry,President and COO; John Ball, Executive VP, Operations & Administration; John Harris, CFO

IDG Books Technology Publishing Group: Richard Swadley, Senior Vice President and Publisher; Mary Bednarek, Vice President and Publisher, Networking and Certification; Walter R. Bruce III, Vice President and Publisher, General User and Design Professional; Joseph Wikert, Vice President and Publisher, Programming; Mary C. Corder, Editorial Director, Branded Technology Editorial; Andy Cummings, Publishing Director, General User and Design Professional; Barry Pruett, Publishing Director, Visual

IDG Books Manufacturing: Ivor Parker, Vice President, Manufacturing

IDG Books Marketing: John Helmus, Assistant Vice President, Director of Marketing

IDG Books Online Management: Brenda McLaughlin, Executive Vice President, Chief Internet Officer; Gary Millrood, Executive Vice President of Business Development, Sales and Marketing

IDG Books Packaging: Marc J. Mikulich, Vice President, Brand Strategy and Research

IDG Books Production for Branded Press: Debbie Stailey, Production Director

IDG Books Sales: Roland Elgey, Senior Vice President, Sales and Marketing; Michael Violano, Vice President, International Sales and Sub Rights

♦

The publisher would like to give special thanks to Patrick J. McGovern, without whom this book would not have been possible.

♦

Contents at a Glance

Table of Contents

Dreamweaver 4

Dreamweaver 4 is the industry standard for Web site design and production. The program's flexible interface provides simultaneous graphical and HTML editing — you can lay out pages like an artist, but you can fine-tune the associated code like a programmer. And Dreamweaver's built-in FTP features let you upload your site to the Web in a snap — so that you can share your masterpieces with the world.

In this part . . .

- What You See
- The Basics
- What You Can Do

What You See: The Document Window

Your primary workspace in Dreamweaver 4 is the Document window. In the Document window, you construct your individual Web pages using panels, inspectors, and dialog boxes to format your work. You can view the Document

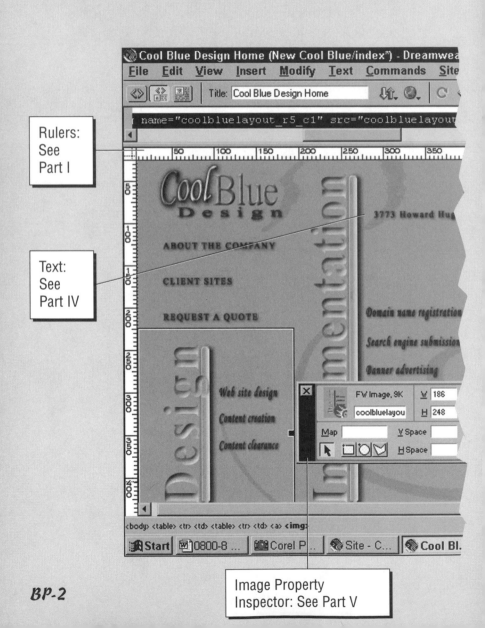

Rulers:
See
Part I

Text:
See
Part IV

Image Property
Inspector: See Part V

window full screen to work in a completely graphical environment, or you can choose the Split View (shown here) where you can view the Document window and the HTML source code for your page at the same time. For details on working with each of the features shown here, check out the associated part later in this book.

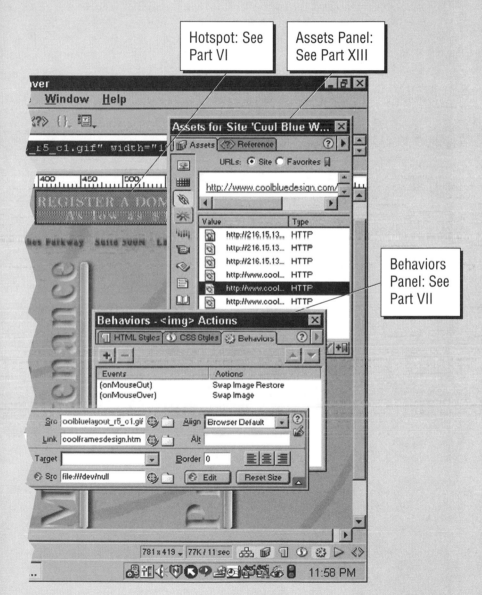

Hotspot: See Part VI

Assets Panel: See Part XIII

Behaviors Panel: See Part VII

What You See: The Site Window

In the Site window, you can examine your entire site. Here, you can view a list of all files in your site and a map of how those files connect together. The Site window is also where you connect to the host server so that you can transfer your site from your local computer to the Web.

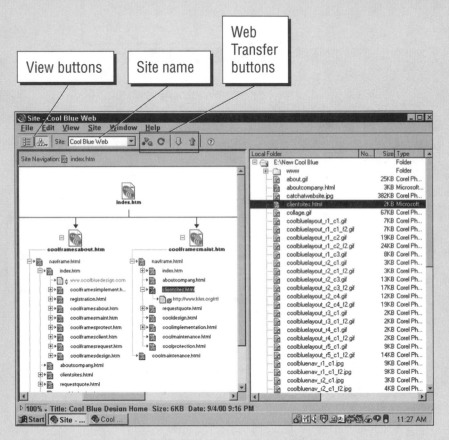

Toolbar Tables

Dreamweaver provides you with a number of View buttons where you can open different views of your site. You can easily switch among views to examine your site in different ways. Each Dreamweaver view offers specialized menus and tools to help you perform your work in that view. Certain views are available for an individual document or page, while other views are available for the entire site. At any time while you work, you can choose to preview your site in target Web browsers to see your site from the user's perspective.

 When you have several documents open in a site, you can select which document you want to work on by clicking the icon's name in the Windows status bar at the bottom of the screen. You can also select the Site button to work on the entire site.

 The buttons in the bottom-right corner of the Document window — Show Site, Show Assets, Show HTML Styles, Show CSS Styles, Show Behaviors, Show History, and Show Code inspector — are collectively known as the Mini-Launcher because you can click these buttons to open their respective panels. You can also display the full-size Launcher, a window for doing the same thing but that floats freely in the Document window, by choosing Window⇨Launcher from the Menu bar.

Site buttons and tools

Button/Tool	Name	What You Can Do
	Site Files button	View a list of all documents and dependent files in your site
	Map Only button	View a map showing icons representing all your documents and their relationship
	Connects to remote host button	Connects your local computer and your Web host, allowing you to transfer files between the two computers
	Get File(s) button	Download (retrieve) documents and files from the host
	Put File(s) button	Upload (send) documents and files to the host

Document buttons and tools

Button/Tool	Name	What You Can Do
	Show Code View button	View HTML page code full screen
	Show Code and Design View button	View HTML page code and Document window at the same time
	Show Design View button	View Document window full screen
	File Management button	Click and then select Get to retrieve files from the Web site host or select Put to send files to the host
	Preview/Debug in Browser button	Click and select to preview or debug in IE or Navigator
	Reference button	Click to open the Reference panel for CSS, HTML, and JavaScript assistance
	View Options button	Click to select tools (such as Visual Aids and the Ruler) to assist you in viewing your site
	Show Site icon	Switch to Site View
	Show Assets icon	Open the Assets panel
	Show HTML Styles icon	Open the HTML Styles panel
	Show CSS Styles icon	Open the CSS Styles panel
	Show Behaviors icon	Open the Behaviors panel
	Show History icon	Open the History panel
	Show Code Inspector icon	Open a separate window showing HTML source code. HTML and JavaScript are color-coded.

The Basics: Displaying Views

You can work with content in your Document window using either the Standard View or the Layout View. If you've used a previous version of Dreamweaver, you'll recognize the *Standard View* as the familiar — and only — WYSIWYG ("what you see is what you get") graphical view through which you lay out pages in the Document window.

The *Layout View* is new to Dreamweaver 4 and is specifically geared toward helping you design your Web page using tables. The advantage of the Layout View is that it provides a simpler interface for drawing and editing tables and table cells. Two special tools are available only when working in Layout View: the Draw Layout Cell button and the Draw Layout Table button, both located in the Layout area of the Common Objects panel.

> **TIP**
> If the Common Objects panel does not show, choose Window⇨Objects from the Menu bar.

 To work in Standard View: Select the document you want to work on. Click the Standard View button in the View area of the Common Objects panel.

 To work in Layout View: Select the document you want to work on. Click the Layout View button in the View area of the Common Objects panel.

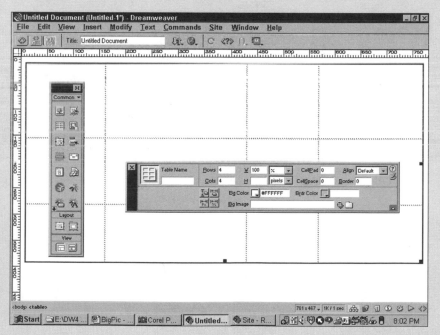

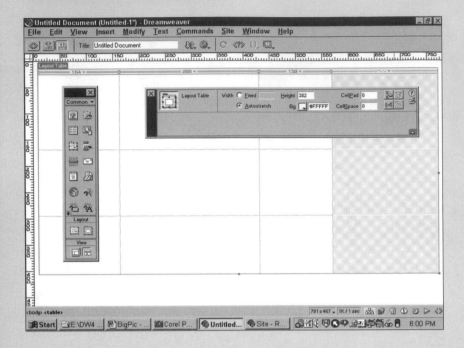

 Dreamweaver offers a number of view options you can select to speed your work in the Document window. These include options to display rulers, a grid, and a tracing image — an image you can import from a graphics program and use as a blueprint for designing a page. View options also include visual aids, such as table borders and invisible elements — yellow markers in the Document window that represent page objects, such as layers and named anchors.

 Turn on view options in the Document window by clicking the View Options button and choosing from the resulting menu.

The Basics: Using Panels, Property Inspectors, and Dialog Boxes

Dreamweaver panels, property inspectors, and dialog boxes provide you with a way to enter details about all aspects of your Dreamweaver site. These interfaces offer areas where you can add and format page features, set up navigation and behaviors, and manage your workflow.

Panels

A *panel* typically provides information about all instances of a particular page feature. For example, the Layers panel lists information about all the layers on the current page. One panel you may find very helpful is the Objects panel, which lets you add features, such as images, tables, and media to your pages without accessing menus. The Objects panel is actually seven panels combined into one. To work with a different Objects panel, you simply click the Panel selector located at the top of the Objects panel and select a new panel from the pop-up menu.

You can open panels by choosing Window from the Menu bar and then selecting the desired panel name — such as Behaviors, Frames, or Layers — from the drop-down list. Panels can remain open in the Document window for as long as you want. To close a panel, simply click its close (X) button.

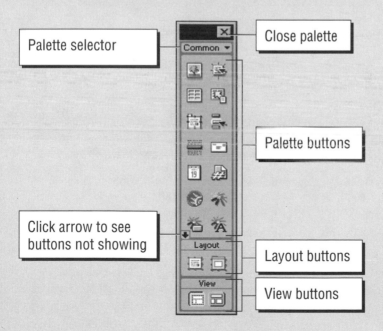

Palette selector

Close palette

Palette buttons

Click arrow to see buttons not showing

Layout buttons

View buttons

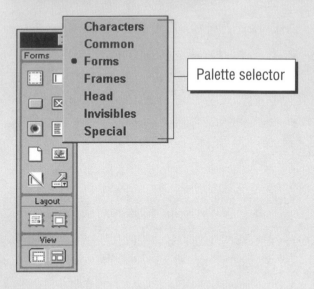

Palette selector

Property inspectors

A *Property inspector* is unique to the individual document object it represents and contains details on attributes of the object. For example, selecting text on a page opens the Text Property inspector where you can format the text size, font, color, link, and other information. To make certain that the Property inspectors show in the Document window, choose Window⇨Properties from the Menu bar.

 Each Property inspector has a small down arrow in the lower-right corner, called an Expander button. Click the button to enlarge the Property inspector to view additional formatting options. In an expanded Property inspector, click the small up arrow in the lower-right corner to collapse the inspector.

 The pencil-and-paper button at the right of each Property inspector provides you access to the Quick Tag Editor. Click this button to open the Quick Tag Editor to open a work area where you can hand-code HTML for the selected object. When you are done, click outside the Quick Tag Editor work area to apply your edits to the HTML page code.

Dialog boxes

Dialog boxes appear when you must enter additional information about a page object or action. Dialog boxes do not stay open in the Document window while you work — they vanish after you enter and submit the needed information or click the Cancel button.

 TIP Use underlining shortcuts in Dreamweaver to speed your work. For example, if a field name in a dialog box or a menu selection has an underlined letter, such as Text, just press the Alt key plus that letter to select that field or menu item.

The Basics: Getting Help

Dreamweaver offers a variety of tools to help you find the answer to virtually any question you have about the program. The Help tools provide basic information for beginners as well as advanced references detailing HTML and JavaScript code.

 You can get help working with any panel or Property inspector by clicking the Help button — the small question mark — in the top-right corner of the current panel or inspector.

You can also access help using the Help menu at the Menu bar. Just choose Help and then select one of the following options:

✔ **Using Dreamweaver:** Provides definitions and itemized steps in performing routine Dreamweaver tasks. Opens in the Microsoft Internet Explorer browser and contains Help Contents, Index, and Search categories.

 ✔ **Reference:** Opens a panel offering a dictionary-style reference on CSS, HTML, and JavaScript. You can also access the Reference panel by clicking the Reference button in the Document window.

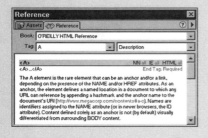

✔ **Dreamweaver Exchange, Dreamweaver Support Center, and Macromedia Online Forms:** Connects you to the Web where you can find constantly updated information on working with Dreamweaver, answers to Frequently Asked Questions, and program extensions. You can also join a developer's forum where you can chat with other Dreamweaver users to get (and give) help.

✔ **Extending Dreamweaver:** Provides assistance in performing more advanced Dreamweaver tasks, especially tasks involving the integration of adjunct programs, such as Flash, with Dreamweaver. Opens in the Microsoft Internet Explorer browser and contains Help Contents, Index, and Search categories.

The Basics: Starting Dreamweaver

Each time you start Dreamweaver, a new Untitled document opens in the Document window. Starting Dreamweaver also opens the site you were working on when you last exited (Windows) or quit (Macintosh) the program. Follow these steps to start Dreamweaver:

In Windows: Choose Start⇨Programs⇨Macromedia Dreamweaver 4⇨ Dreamweaver 4 from the Status Bar at the bottom of Windows.

In Macintosh: Click the Application button on the Launcher and then click the Dreamweaver program icon.

 Don't get confused between the Macintosh Launcher and the Dreamweaver Launcher — they are not the same!

Opening a new site

Opening a new site means creating a new location where your documents (Web pages) and dependent files (such as images and audio files) are stored. You can open a new site in any view as follows:

1. Create a new folder on your computer and name it. For example, you can name the folder for your first site, **My First Site.**

2. Start Dreamweaver and choose Site⇨New Site from the Menu bar.

3. At the Site Definition dialog box, enter a name for your site at the Site Name text box. The name can be the same as the site folder you created in Step 1.

4. In the Local Root Folder area, click the folder button and browse to locate the site folder you created in Step 1.

5. Click OK.

Opening a new document

Opening a new document means creating a new Web page to save in your site folder. Create a new document using either of these methods:

✔ In the Document window, choose File⇨New from the Menu bar.

✔ In Site Files View, choose File⇨New File from the Menu bar.

Saving a document

After opening a new document or editing an existing document, you must save your work. A document must be saved in your site folder before it can be uploaded, or sent, from your computer to a host computer for display on the Web. To save an open document, follow these steps:

1. Choose File⇨Save from the Menu bar.

2. At the Save As dialog box, browse to your site folder at the Save In drop-down list (this folder may already be selected).

3. In the File Name area, enter a name for your document followed by the extension .html.

4. Click Save.

Saving a site

To save a site, you can simply save each document contained in the site. Also save all dependent files, such as images, that you use in your documents.

The Basics: Developing Your First Page

Developing a Web page from scratch is an easy task with Dreamweaver. Here's a 5-minute procedure for creating a Web page (start your stopwatch . . . now!):

1. Start Dreamweaver. *See also* "Starting Dreamweaver" earlier in this part. Starting the program creates a new untitled document.

2. Open a new site. *See also* "Opening a New Site" earlier in this part.

3. Switch to the Untitled document. In Windows, click the Untitled Document button in the taskbar. On a Macintosh, click the Untitled Document window.

4. Add content and color to your page by doing as many (or as few) of the following procedures as you want:

   - **Choose a background color:** Choose Modify⇨Page Properties from the Menu bar. Click the Background color swatch and then select a color from the palette. Click OK.

   - **Name the page:** Enter a name for your page in the Title text box at the top of the Document window.

   - **Enter text:** Click your cursor in the Document window and enter something compelling, riveting, or insightful. Or just tap your fingers randomly on the keyboard. Include the sentence, "I just bought this great book from IDG Books Worldwide, Inc."

   - **Create a link:** Select the text, "IDG Books Worldwide, Inc." A Text Property inspector appears (if it doesn't, choose Window⇨Properties from the Menu bar). In the Link text box, type **www.idgbooks.com**.

   - **Add an image:** Click the Insert Image button on the Common Objects panel (if the panel doesn't show, open it by choosing Window⇨Objects from the Menu bar). Browse to find a GIF or JPEG image on your computer and click Select.

5. Save your document. *See also* "Saving a Document" earlier in this part.

6. Preview the page in a Web browser. Click the Preview in Browser button in the Document window. (Alternatively, you can choose File⇨Preview in Browser from the Menu bar.) From the menu, select an option for the browser you want to preview the page in. If you go online, you can click your IDG Books Worldwide, Inc. link to check that it actually opens the IDG Books Worldwide, Inc. Web site. Click the Back button in your browser to return to your page.

What You Can Do: Create an Informational Site

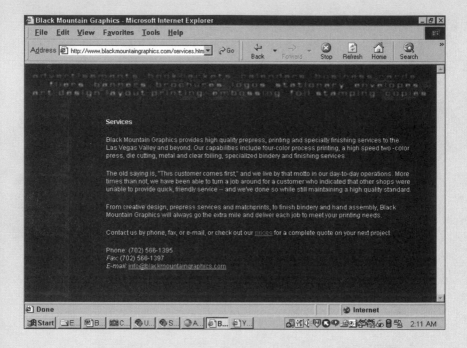

Dreamweaver excels at making the Web page designer's job as painless as possible. Dreamweaver helps beginners design simple, text-based sites, and it also helps advanced designers perform the drudgery of maintaining text-intensive sites that require frequent updating. To create an informational site, you can

Get started by

Creating Basic Web Pages, Part I

Putting Words on a Page, Part IV

Building Navigation and Activity, Part VII

Enhance your design by

Constructing Pages with Tables, Part III

Structuring Pages with Frames Part X

Get your site on the Web by

Mapping Your Entire Site, Part XII

Publishing and Updating Your Site, Part XIV

What You Can Do: Create a Web Photo Album

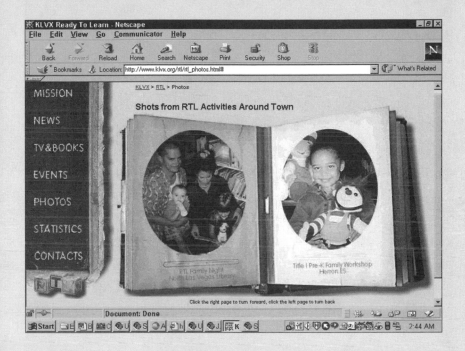

Whether you're an individual wanting to share photos with distant family members or a company seeking to publicize its latest work, images can help you tell your story more effectively. By using layers and behaviors, you can stack multiple photos on your Web page and offer users a way to *turn* album pages with a click of the mouse. Instead of photos, you may even consider offering short video or audio clips or streaming media to reach your audience. You may also choose to create a more elegant navigation bar for your site that includes rollovers, an image map, or Flash buttons.

Get started by

Creating Basic Web Pages, Part I

Laying Out Pages with Layers, Part II

Working with Images, Part V

Enhance your design by

Incorporating Interactive Images, Part VI

Building Navigation and Activity, Part VII

Adding Multimedia Elements, Part IX

Get your site on the Web by

Mapping Your Entire Site, Part XII

Publishing and Updating Your Site, Part XIV

 Dreamweaver offers a built-in command for creating a simplified Web photo album. By choosing Commands⇨Create Web Photo Album, you can turn a folder of images into a Web page, showing thumbnails of all the images. Users can click any thumbnail to view the full-size original image.

What You Can Do: Run a Web Store

From Star Trek Tribbles to antique lockets, everyone seems to be selling something on the Web . . . why not you? Creating a Web store requires that you create a catalog of your products, provide users with shopping carts to track their selected products, conduct secure credit card transactions, and coordinate shipping of the goods to the buyer. Dreamweaver can help you set up the storefront (build the catalog) and construct customer information forms. Dreamweaver can also assist you in managing the large number of images characteristic of store sites via the Assets panel. However, you must work outside of Dreamweaver to develop the necessary perl or CGI scripts (computer programming code) to complete the rest of the site (or else buy prewritten code from a third-party vendor). You can then return to Dreamweaver to tweak the HTML code to call your programming scripts. Lastly, you want to include descriptive <meta> tags so that search engines can catalog and direct Web traffic to your site. Here's how to get your store site online and your merchandise moving:

The Big Picture: Dreamweaver 4

Get started by

Enhance your design and workflow by

Get your site on the Web by

Part I

Creating Basic Web Pages

The most significant — and fortunately the easiest — process in building a Web site is creating the individual pages that convey the site's content. Even if you plan on creating an ultra-hip site chock full of animation and interactive forms, the vast majority of your site-building efforts are spent constructing basic Web pages comprised of words and images. This part shows you how to set up, color, and name individual Web pages. You also discover how to add basic elements such as text, graphics, and tables to your pages.

In this part . . .

Adjusting Page Size

When you design Web pages, you must consider how your target audiences will view them. People looking at your page may view it at any number of screen resolutions from 640 x 480 all the way up to 1024 x 768. They may even view your pages using WebTV. Because pages appear differently at different resolutions, Dreamweaver offers you the ability to build your pages for a variety of monitor resolutions. The higher the resolution, the larger the workspace in your Document window.

To size your pages, click the Window Size Indicator in the Status bar (*see also* "The Big Picture") and select a size from the pop-up menu.

You can select from any predefined window size or select the Edit Sizes option to open the Preferences dialog box where you can enter and save any height and width dimensions you want. Dreamweaver sizes the page to your selected dimensions and creates the associated HTML code for the page.

Depending on how you create your pages, they may or may not resize well at different resolutions. Most people set desktop monitors to 640 x 480 or 800 x 600 and notebook screens to 800 x 600 or 1024 x 768. Therefore, building pages at 800 x 600 is often a safe bet.

Displaying the Current Date and Time

Dreamweaver offers you the option of including the date and time on a Web page, along with the capability of formatting each item in a variety of ways.

Inserting the date and time

To insert the date and time on a page, follow these steps:

1. In the Document window, position the cursor where you want the date to appear on your page.

2. Choose Insert⇨Date from the Menu bar.

Alternatively, you may select the Insert Date button from the Common Objects panel. Doing so opens the Insert Date dialog box.

3. Select a Day Format and a Date Format from the drop-down lists.

4. (Optional) Select a Time Format from the drop-down list.

5. Click OK.

Dreamweaver adds the date and time (if you chose to add a time stamp) to the page and creates the associated HTML code.

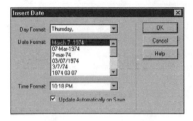

 Click to check the Update Automatically on Save box if you want the inserted date and time to refresh each time you save the page.

Deleting the date and time

To delete a date and time stamp from a page, click and drag to select the text of the date and time stamp and then press the Backspace or Delete key. Dreamweaver removes the stamp from your page and deletes the associated code in the HTML for the page.

Entering Text

You can enter and manipulate text on a Web page in Dreamweaver by using similar procedures to those you use when working with a word processing document.

Inserting text

To enter text on a page, click your mouse in the Document window and begin typing. Your mouse pointer appears as a blinking cursor that moves along with the text you enter. When you reach the end of a line, the text automatically wraps to the next line. (To create a line break, *see also* "Inserting or Deleting Line Breaks" in this part.) Dreamweaver automatically adds the associated code for your new text in the HTML for the page.

Deleting text

To delete text from a page, in the Document window select the text that you want to delete and press Backspace or Delete on your keyboard. Dreamweaver deletes the text from the page and from the associated code in the HTML.

Modifying text — quick and easy

You can modify how text appears on a page by editing its font, size, color, alignment, and other attributes.

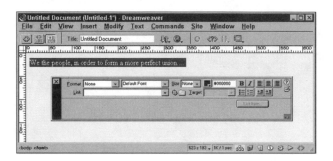

Modify text by clicking in the Document window and dragging your mouse to select the text you want to modify. Doing so opens the Text Property inspector. If the Property inspector does not show, choose Window⇨Properties from the Menu bar to open it. On the Text Property inspector, modify any of the following properties:

✔ **Format:** From the first drop-down list, select a default text style. These styles are relative, not absolute. Heading 1 is the largest style and Heading 6 is the smallest, but none of the headings correlate with a specific pixel size. Select a text font from the second drop-down list. Browsers show your text formatted as the first font in your selection that resides on the user's computer.

✔ **Color:** Click the color box next to each property and select a text color from the Web-safe color palette that appears. Alternatively, you may enter a hexadecimal color code directly in any color code box. You can set the default text color in the Page Properties dialog box for the page. *See also* "Establishing Page Properties."

✔ **Bold or Italic:** Click the Bold button to boldface your selected text. Click the Italic button to italicize your selected text. You can click either button or both.

✔ **Alignment:** Click an alignment button to align your text. Choices are Left, Center, and Right.

Dreamweaver automatically adds the associated code for your text modifications in the HTML for the page.

Establishing Page Properties

The Page Properties dialog box provides you control over how several key page properties appear, including the title of the page, page background color, link colors, and page margins. Selections apply only to the current page, not to the entire site. Open the Page Properties dialog box by choosing Modify➪Page Properties from the Menu bar. Then make changes to any of the following:

- ✔ **Title:** Enter a page title in the box. This title appears in the Title Bar area of the page during construction in Dreamweaver and when the page is viewed through a Web browser.

- ✔ **Background Image:** Click Browse (Windows) or Choose (Macintosh) to locate the image file that you want to appear as the Document window background. If the image is smaller than the available background area, it repeats in checkerboard fashion to completely fill the background.

- ✔ **Background, Text, Links, Visited Links, and Active Links:** Click the color box next to each property and select a color from the Web-safe color palette that appears. Alternatively, you may enter a hexadecimal color code directly in any color code box.

- ✔ **Left Margin and Top Margin:** These property boxes set up margins that affect how your page appears in Microsoft Internet Explorer. Enter a whole number for the number of pixels of standoff space you want on the left and top sides of your document.

- ✔ **Margin Width and Margin Height:** These property boxes set up margins that affect how your page appears in Netscape Navigator. Enter a whole number for the number of pixels of standoff space you want on the left and top sides of your document.

- ✔ **Document Encoding:** Choose a language for character encoding of text on your page. Click Reload to display the page with the changed encoding.

- ✔ **Tracing Image:** Click Browse (Windows) or Choose (Macintosh) to locate the image file you want to use as a guide for laying out your Web page in the Document window.

- ✔ **Image Transparency:** Drag the slider to adjust the visibility level of the tracing image. At 0% the tracing image is invisible, while at 100% the image is completely opaque.

Click Apply to view the effect of any property you change. Click OK to accept your changes and close the Page Properties dialog box. Dreamweaver shows the page properties you selected and creates the associated HTML code for the page.

Even if you choose to use a background image, go ahead and select a complementary background color — the color shows while the background image is downloading.

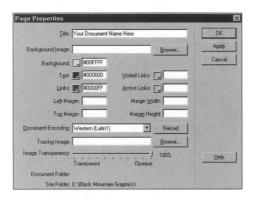

Guiding Your Work in the Document Window

Dreamweaver offers you complete control over how you work in the Document window by providing two guide tools — rulers and a grid — to help you accurately lay out your work. You can customize a variety of guide tool attributes, such as ruler increments and grid snapping, to suit your personal preferences and speed Web page development.

Turning rulers on and off

Using rulers in the Document window can help you measure and numerically position page elements. Toggle the Ruler on and off by choosing View⇨Rulers⇨Show from the Menu bar.

Moving and resetting the origin

By default, the origin, or (0,0) coordinate of a Dreamweaver ruler is set to the upper-left corner of the Document window. Reposition it to any coordinate in the Document window by clicking the origin crosshairs and dragging them to new coordinates. Reset the origin to its default position by choosing View⇨Rulers⇨Reset Origin from the Menu bar.

Changing ruler measurement units

You can change the ruler's measuring increment by choosing View⇨Rulers from the Menu bar and then choosing Pixels, Inches, or Centimeters from the pop-up menu.

Viewing the grid

Dreamweaver provides a Document window grid that can assist you in visually positioning and aligning page elements. You can toggle the grid on and off by choosing View⇨Grid⇨Show Grid from the Menu bar.

Activating and deactivating grid snapping

The Document window grid offers a snapping feature that causes a page element to automatically align precisely with the snap-to points you define. You can toggle grid snapping on and off by choosing View⇨Grid⇨Snap To Grid from the Menu bar.

Changing grid settings

You can adjust how the grid appears in the Document window through the Grid Settings dialog box.

Open the Grid Settings dialog box by choosing View⇨Grid⇨Edit Grid from the Menu bar and change any of the following attributes:

- ✔ **Color:** Click the color box and select a new color for the grid-lines from the Web-safe color palette that appears. Alternatively, you may enter a color code directly in the color code box.

- ✔ **Show Grid:** Click the check box to turn on the grid. Click again to uncheck the box to turn off the grid.

- ✔ **Snap to Grid:** Click the check box to turn on snapping. Click to uncheck the box to turn off grid snapping.

- ✔ **Spacing:** Enter a whole number in the box for the spacing between gridlines (the minimum is 25) and select a measurement increment from the drop-down list.

🖝 **Display:** Click a radio button to draw gridlines as either lines or dots.

Click Apply to view the effect of any attribute you change. Click OK to accept your changes and close the dialog box.

Inserting or Deleting Line Breaks

 When you enter text in a word processing program, pressing Enter (Windows) or Return (Macintosh) creates a line break — your cursor moves to the start of the next line. However, when you enter text in the Dreamweaver Document window, pressing Enter or Return instead creates a paragraph break. (*See also* Part II.)

Inserting a line break

To insert a line break on a page, choose Insert⇨Special Characters⇨ Line Break from the Menu bar or press Shift+Enter (Windows) or Shift+Return (Macintosh). Alternatively, you may click the Insert Line Break button from the Character Objects panel. If the panel doesn't show, open it by choosing Window⇨Objects from the Menu bar. Dreamweaver places the cursor at the start of the next line and creates the line break HTML code for the page.

Deleting a line break

To delete a break from a page, place the cursor at the beginning of the line immediately following the line break and press the Backspace key. Dreamweaver removes the break from your page and deletes the associated code in the HTML for the page.

Manipulating Horizontal Rules

Horizontal rules are lines that create visual breaks between content on a Web page. These lines help visitors logically group the information they see on the page.

 ### Inserting a horizontal rule

To insert a horizontal rule on a page, choose Insert⇨Horizontal Rule from the Menu bar. Alternatively, you may select the Insert Horizontal Rule button from the Common Objects panel. (When you insert a horizontal rule), if the panel doesn't show, open it by choosing Window⇨Objects from the Menu bar. Dreamweaver places the rule on your page and creates the associated code in the HTML for the page.

Deleting a horizontal rule

To delete a horizontal rule from a page, click the horizontal rule in the Document window and press the Delete key on your keyboard. Dreamweaver removes the rule from your page and deletes the associated code in the HTML for the page.

Modifying a horizontal rule

You can modify how a horizontal rule appears on page by editing its dimensions, alignment, or shading.

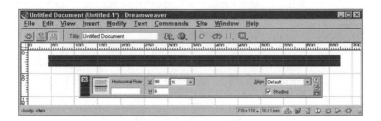

To modify a horizontal rule, click the rule in the Document window to open the Horizontal Rule Property inspector. If the Property inspector does not show, choose Window➪Properties from the Menu bar to open it. Modify any of the following properties:

- 🖝 **W** and **H:** Click the arrow button to specify the dimension measurements of the rule. Choose pixels to measure an absolute value or choose % to measure as a percentage of the Web page. Then enter a number for the width in the W box and a number for the height in the H box. (*Note:* If a rule width measured in pixels is larger than the Document window width, the rule appears only as wide as the Document window.)

- 🖝 **Align:** Click the arrow button and choose an alignment from the drop-down list. Choices are Default, Left, Center, and Right.

- 🖝 **Shading:** Click the check box to shade the horizontal rule. Leave the check box unchecked to make the rule a solid line.

Manipulating Images

Next to entering text, manipulating images on a Web page is probably the most common Dreamweaver function you perform. You can add or delete an image and modify its properties to create an aesthetically pleasing layout that effectively conveys the information you want to deliver to the user.

Inserting an image

To insert an image on a page, follow these steps:

1. Choose Insert⇨Image from the Menu bar.

   Alternatively, you may click the Insert Image button from the Common Objects panel. If the panel doesn't show, open it by choosing Window⇨Objects from the Menu bar.

2. At the Select Image Source dialog box, click the image you want to insert.

   If the image is outside the current folder, click the arrow tab beside the Look In box and browse to select the file you want.

3. Click the Select button to insert the image.

   Note: Every image you want to include on a Web page must reside within the folder of the current site. If you attempt to insert an image from another location, Dreamweaver asks whether you want to copy the image to the current site root. Click Yes. At the Copy File As dialog box, you can enter a new name for the image in the File Name box, or you can accept the current name and click Save.

Dreamweaver places the image on your page and creates a reference to the file in the HTML code for the page.

Click the Preview check box at the bottom of the Select Image Source dialog box to view a thumbnail of an image before you select it for insertion. The preview area also tells you the size of the image and the expected download time.

Deleting an image

To delete an image from a page, click the image in the Document window and press the Delete key on your keyboard. Dreamweaver removes the rule from your page and deletes the associated code in the HTML code for the page.

Modifying an image — quick and easy

You can modify how an image appears on a page by editing its size and alignment, adding a border, and changing other attributes.

To modify an image, click the image in the Document window to select it. If the Property inspector does not appear, choose Window⇨Properties from the Menu bar to open it. Modify any of the following properties:

✔ **Resize the image:** Click and drag a sizing handle to change the dimensions of the image. To resize the image maintaining the same proportions, hold down the Shift key as you drag a sizing handle.

✔ **Align the image:** On the Image Property inspector, click an Alignment button to position the image on the page (or within a cell if the image is located in a table cell). Alignment button choices consist of Left, Center, and Right.

✔ **Add a border to the image:** On the Image Property inspector, enter a number in the Border box to add a border of that thickness to the image. Border thickness is measured in pixels.

Sizing handle   Border Thickness box

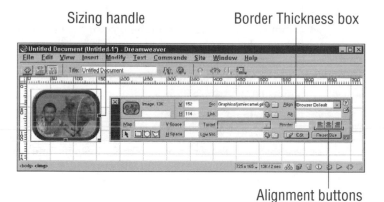

Alignment buttons

When your modification is made, Dreamweaver also modifies the associated code in the HTML for the page.

For thorough coverage on positioning, resizing, and performing other functions on your image, *see also* Part V.

Dreamweaver doesn't offer image-editing functions, such as recoloring or adding drop shadows — you have to use a program such as Macromedia Fireworks or Adobe Photoshop to accomplish these tasks.

Setting Up a Table

Adding a table to a Web page can help you lay out page elements more easily in the Document window. Tables consist of as many holding areas, or *cells,* as you want, and you can place virtually any Web element, such as text or an image, into a cell. Cells are organized horizontally into *rows* and vertically into *columns.* Dreamweaver provides you with complete control over the size, position, color, and other attributes of your table. And you can edit these attributes at any time via the Table Property inspector.

Inserting a Table

To add a table, choose Insert➪Table from the Menu bar to open the Insert Table dialog box. Alternatively, you may click the Insert Table button from the Common Objects panel. If the panel doesn't show, open it by choosing Window➪Objects from the Menu bar. Enter the following information in the dialog box:

- ✔ **Rows:** Enter a number in the box for the number of rows in the table.

- ✔ **Columns:** Enter a number in the box for the number of columns in the table.

- ✔ **Cell Padding:** Enter a number in the box specifying how many pixels of padding you want between the inside edge of a cell and its contents.

- ✔ **Cell Spacing:** Enter a number in the box specifying how many pixels separation you want between cells.

- ✔ **Width:** Select Percent from the drop-down list and then enter a number (0 - 100) in the box for the percent of page width you want the entire table to occupy. Or select Pixels from the drop-down list and enter a number of pixels for the width of the entire table.

- ✔ **Border:** Enter a number in the box for the width of the table borders in pixels. Entering 0 causes the borders to disappear.

Dreamweaver adds the table to the page and creates the associated HTML code.

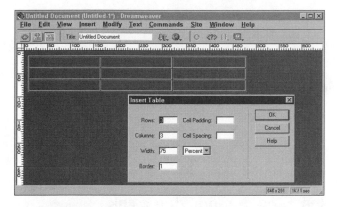

Deleting a table

To delete a table from a page, click the border of the table to select it and then press the Backspace or Delete key. Dreamweaver removes the table from your page and deletes the associated code in the HTML for the page.

For thorough coverage on working with tables, *see also* Part III.

Storing Information in Table Cells

After you insert a table on a page, you can add or delete elements, such as text and images, in the table cells. Dreamweaver modifies the associated code in the HTML for each table element you add or delete.

Adding an image to a cell

To add an image to a table cell, click to position the cursor in a table cell and choose Insert⇔Image from the Menu bar. Browse and select an image you want to add to the cell and then click Select. *See also* "Inserting an Image" earlier in this part.

Adding text to a cell

To add text to a table cell, click to position the cursor in a table cell and type the text you want placed inside the cell.

Deleting an image from a cell

To delete an image from a table cell, select the image and press Backspace or Delete.

Deleting text from a cell

To delete text from a table cell, select the text and press Backspace or Delete.

Working with Links

Linking your page to other Web pages enables you to direct visitors to related content on the Web. To insert a link, you must specify an image or some text to serve as the link and the location where you want the link to go. The link can go to another page within your site or to another page elsewhere on the Web.

Inserting or modifying a link

To insert a link on a page, follow these steps:

1. Select the text or image you want to make a link.

   Doing so opens the Property inspector for your text or image. If the Property inspector does not show, choose Window⇨ Properties from the Menu bar to open it.

2. In the Link area of the Property inspector, enter the name of the new link or enter the name of a different link.

   Alternatively, you may browse to select a link at the Select File dialog box and click Select. The link can be another page in your site or a URL.

3. The link is created. Dreamweaver adds the associated code in the HTML for the page.

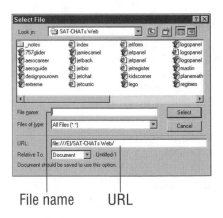

File name   URL

Deleting a link

To delete a link from a page, follow these steps:

1. Select the text or image you want to remove the link from.

   Doing so opens the Property inspector for your text or image. If the Properties inspector does not show, choose Window⇨ Properties from the Menu bar to open it.

2. In the Property inspector, delete the name of the link from the Link box.

The link is removed. Dreamweaver removes the associated code in the HTML for the page.

Part II

Laying Out Pages with Layers

Layers are a key component of Dreamweaver's WYSIWYG (what-you-see-is-what-you-get) interface. Layers enable you to partition off rectangular regions of the Document window and put anything you inside the regions. Most importantly, you can easily position and reposition the regions anywhere you want in the Document window.

In this part . . .

Adding a Layer

Add a layer to the workspace of your Document window by using one of the following methods:

- ✔ Choose Insert⇨Layer from the Menu bar. A new layer of default size and position appears in the upper-left corner of your Document window. (*See also* Part XIII for details on setting layer defaults.)

- ✔ Click the Draw Layer button from the Common Objects panel and drag it into the Document window. If the panel does not show, open it by choosing Window⇨Objects from the Menu bar. A new layer of default size and position appears in the upper left-hand corner of your Document window. (*See also* Part XIII for details on setting layer defaults.)

- ✔ Click the Draw Layer button from the Common Objects panel. Position the crosshair cursor anywhere in your Document window and then click and drag until the layer obtains the dimensions you want. Release the mouse button.

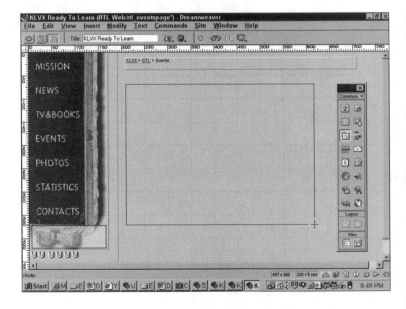

Here's an easy way to draw a layer and set its dimensions: Click the Draw Layer button from the Common Objects panel. Position the crosshair cursor anywhere in your Document window and then click and drag until the layer obtains the dimensions you want.

Dreamweaver adds the associated code for the layer to the HTML source code for your page.

For each layer you draw, Dreamweaver places a layer marker in the upper-left corner of the Document window. For CSS layers (applicable to both Internet Explorer and Netscape Navigator), the marker appears as the letter *C* in a yellow box. For Netscape layers (the layer formatting unique to Navigator), the marker appears as the letter *N* in a yellow box.

Aligning Layers

Aligning layers can help you precisely lay out visual content in the Document window. You can align layers by the top, left side, right side, or bottom.

To align layers, select the layers you want to align by pressing and holding the Shift key and then clicking each layer in the Document window. Choose Modify⇨Align from the Menu bar and choose one of the following from the menu that appears:

- ✓ **Left:** Assigns all selected layers the x-coordinate of the leftmost selected layer.

- ✓ **Right:** Aligns the right side of all selected layers with the right side of the rightmost selected layer.

- ✓ **Top:** Assigns all selected layers the y coordinate of the topmost selected layer.

- ✓ **Bottom:** Aligns the bottom of all selected layers with the bottom of the bottommost selected layer.

Dreamweaver changes the associated code for the layers' positions to the HTML source code for your page.

Changing the Visibility of a Layer

You can set whether a layer is *visible* or *hidden* when a Web page loads — first appears — and as a result of specific actions by the user. Visibility can change as many times as you want. (*See also* Part VII for additional information on assigning behaviors to control the visibility of a layer.) Visibility options consist of:

- ✔ **Default:** The layer's initial visibility is the default setting. *See also* Part XIII for details on setting layer defaults.

- ✔ **Inherit:** For a nested layer, the layer's initial visibility is the same visibility of its parent. For an unnested layer, selecting the inherit option causes the layer to appear as visible.

- ✔ **Visible:** The layer's initial visibility is visible.

- ✔ **Hidden:** The layer's initial visibility is hidden.

Layer visibility can be set using either the Layer Property inspector or the Layers panel.

To set the initial visibility of a layer via the Layer Property inspector, select the layer in the Document window to open the Layer Property inspector. If the inspector does not show, open it by choosing Window➪Properties from the Menu bar. Click the down arrow tab at the Vis box and choose a visibility option from the drop-down list.

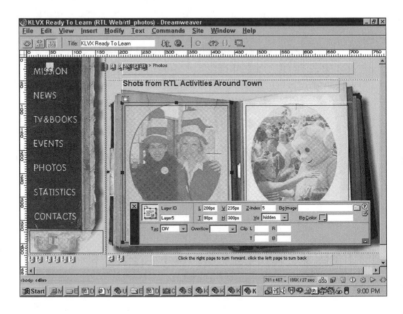

To set the visibility of a layer via the Layers panel:

1. Open the Layers panel by choosing Window⇨Layers from the Menu bar.

2. In the Document window, select the layer for which you want to set the visibility. Alternatively, you can simply click the name of the layer in the Layers panel. The selected layer is highlighted in the Layers panel.

3. Click the Visibility column (the eyeball column) of the selected layer to toggle its visibility. You can toggle among *no eye* (inherit), *open eye* (visible), and *closed eye* (hidden).

Dreamweaver adds the associated code for layer visibility to the HTML source code for your page.

Changing the visibility of multiple layers at the same time

You can set the initial visibility of several layers at the same time by using the Multiple Layers Property inspector. To do so, follow these steps:

1. Press and hold the Shift key while selecting each layer for which you want to change its visibility.

2. If the Multiple Layers Property inspector does not appear, open it by choosing Window⇨Properties from the Menu bar.

3. In the Multiple Layers Property inspector, click the down arrow tab at the Vis box and choose a visibility option from the drop-down list. *See also* "Changing the Visibility of a Layer" earlier in this part for visibility options.

Dreamweaver adds the associated code for layer visibility to the HTML source code for your page.

Converting Layers to Tables

Browsers older than Internet Explorer 4 and Netscape Navigator 4 are unable to properly display pages created with layers. The content may show, but layer positioning and z-index attributes are not interpreted properly. (*See also* "Layering Layers: Setting the Z-index" later in this part for details on z-index.) But that doesn't mean you have to abandon the flexibility of working with layers and revert back to laying out pages with tables. You can ensure

that your Web site reaches the widest audience possible —
including those people who haven't gotten around to updating
their browsers — by using Dreamweaver's Convert Layers to
Tables function. This function enables you to create your pages
with layers and then transform your layout into tables, which are
the more universally accepted browser format.

To convert a page from layers to tables:

1. In the Document window, choose Modify⇨Convert⇨Layers to
   Table from the Menu bar. A Convert Layers to Table dialog box
   appears.

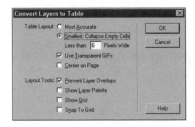

2. In the Convert Layers to Table dialog box, select from the following options:

   • **Most Accurate or Smallest: Collapse Empty Cells:** Click a
     radio button to indicate how accurately you want to lay out
     the table. The Most Accurate option creates a cell for every
     layer and pads the table with additional cells to maintain the
     positioning of the original layers. The Smallest option slightly
     repositions layers to minimize the number of pad cells. Enter
     a number in the Less than: (*number*) Pixels Wide box to indi-
     cate how many pixels of repositioning are allowed.

   • **Use Transparent GIFs:** Check this box to fill the last row of
     the table with transparent GIFs so that all browsers display
     the table identically.

   • **Center on Page:** Check this box to center the resulting table
     on the page. Leave the box unchecked to left justify the
     resulting table.

3. Click OK.

The layers are converted to a table, and Dreamweaver updates the HTML code to reflect the new formatting.

You can easily ignore the Layout Tools area of the Convert Layers to Table dialog box.

When the Use Transparent GIFs box is checked in the Convert Layers to Table dialog box, column widths in the resulting table cannot be edited by dragging column boundaries.

Converting Tables to Layers

After converting a layout from layers to tables, you may decide to reposition content in your Document window. Because repositioning is easier to perform with layers than with tables, you may want to convert your page back to layer formatting. Convert a page layout of tables to layers as follows:

1. In the Document Window, choose Modify⇨Convert⇨Tables to Layers from the Menu bar.

   A Convert Tables to Layers dialog box appears.

2. At the Convert Tables to Layers dialog box, select from the following options:

   • **Prevent Layer Overlaps:** Click the check box to prevent layers from overlapping upon conversion. Overlapping layers do not display properly when viewed in older browsers.

   • **Show Layer Panel:** Click the check box to open the Layers panel upon conversion.

   • **Show Grid:** Click the check box to show the grid in the Document window upon conversion.

   • **Snap To Grid:** Click the check box to cause layers to snap to the Document window grid upon conversion.

3. Click OK.

Each nonempty table cell on the page and all other page elements are converted to layers. Dreamweaver updates the HTML code to reflect the new formatting.

Defining Layer Overflow

Layer overflow refers to how objects in a layer are displayed if the objects exceed the layer boundaries. (*Note:* Layer overflow applies to CSS layers only). Set overflow for a selected layer at the Layer Property inspector by selecting one of the following options:

✔ **Visible:** Expands the layer's boundaries down and to the right so that all the objects contained within are visible.

✔ **Hidden:** Keeps the layer's original boundaries as is. Objects exceeding the layer's boundaries are clipped off.

✔ **Scroll:** Adds scroll bars to the layer whether the objects contained within exceed the layer's boundaries or not. (*Note:* Older browsers may not show the scroll bars.)

✔ **Auto:** Adds scroll bars to the layer only when the objects contained within exceed the layer's boundaries.

Dreamweaver updates the HTML code to reflect the new formatting.

Deleting a Layer

Deleting a layer removes the layer, the layer's contents, and the layer marker from the Document window. To delete a layer, select the layer (*see also* "Selecting a Layer," later in this part) and press Delete or Backspace.

Dreamweaver removes the associated code for the layer and its contents from the HTML source code for your page.

Don't delete a layer if you want to remove it from one page but add it to another. Instead, cut the layer using Edit⇨Cut from the Menu bar. Then open the page where you want to add the layer and choose Edit⇨Paste.

Including a Background Image or Color in a Layer

By default, an unnested layer possesses the same color or background image as the Document window in which it is drawn. Also, a nested child layer possesses the same color or background image as its parent.

You can change the background of any layer by including a background image or color in the layer. Follow these steps:

1. Select the layer where you want to change the background.

2. If the Layer Property inspector does not appear, open it by choosing Window⊃Properties from the Menu bar.

3. In the Layer Property inspector, change one of the following:

   • **Bg Image:** Click the folder to the right of the box and browse to select a background image from the Select Image Source dialog box that appears. Click Select to accept your image choice and close the dialog box. The name of the background image appears in the Bg Image box, and the image is added to the background of the layer.

   • **Bg Color:** Click the color swatch and select a color from the color palette that appears. Alternatively, you can enter a color in the Bg Color box. The new color appears in the background of the selected layer.

Dreamweaver adds the associated code for the layer to the HTML source code for your page.

Layering Layers: Setting the Z-Index

The z-index of a layer indicates its position in a stack of multiple layers. Z-indices are measured in whole numbers and do not have to be consecutive — for example, you can have three layers with z-indices of 1, 3, and 7 respectively. The layer with the largest z-index sits on top of the layer stack, and the layer with the smallest z-index sits on the bottom of the layer stack. Layers with larger z-indices obscure those with smaller z-indices. You can change the z-index of a layer in either the Layer Property inspector or the Layers panel.

To assign the z-index of a layer using the Layer Property inspector: Select the layer to open the Layer Property inspector. If the Layer Property inspector does not show, open it by choosing Window⇨ Properties from the Menu bar. Enter a new number in the Z-Index box of the Layer Property inspector.

To assign the z-index of a layer using the Layers panel:

1. Select the layer to open the Layers panel. (If the Layers panel does not appear, open it by choosing Window⇨Layers from the Menu bar.)

2. Click the Z column for the layer whose z-index you want to change. The current z-index is selected.

3. Enter a new z-index for the layer. The new number appears in the Z column for the selected layer.

To assign relative z-indices to layers by reordering layers in the Layers panel:

1. Open the Layers panel by selecting Window⇨Layers from the Menu bar. The Layers panel lists layers in order of descending z-index.

2. Click the name of a layer for which you want to change its z-index.

3. Drag the layer name into a new list position and release the mouse button. As you drag, the selected layer is indicated by a thick line.

Dreamweaver reorders the list in the Layers panel and renumbers layer z-indices to reflect your change. Also, Dreamweaver updates the associated code for the layers' z-indices in the HTML source code for your page.

Because you don't have to number the z-index of layers consecutively, consider leaving gaps between indices in case you want to add new layers into the middle of the stack. For example, just use even numbers for your indices so that you can easily sandwich a layer with an odd-numbered z-index in between.

Just because a layer has a larger z-index doesn't automatically mean that it obscures a layer with a smaller z-index. Keep in mind that the visibility of a layer — whether it's hidden or visible — also affects which layer the user sees. (*See also* "Changing the Visibility of a Layer," earlier in this part.)

Moving a Layer

You may choose to move a layer to a place in another location in the Document window or to a position relative to the grid or to other objects.

To move a layer, select the layer in the Document window and then reposition your selection by using one of the following three methods:

✔ Click and drag the layer to a new location and release the mouse button.

✔ Click the arrow keys to nudge the layer up, down, left, or right one pixel at a time.

✔ In the Layer Property inspector, enter a new value in the T and L boxes to indicate the pixel coordinates of the layer's top-left corner.

Dreamweaver updates the associated code for the layer's new position in the HTML source code for your page.

Naming a Layer

The first layer you add to a page is automatically named Layer 1, the second layer you add is named Layer 2, and so on. You can change these default number names to other names that help you more easily distinguish layers when working with HTML and when examining layers with the Layer Property inspector or Layers panel.

To name a layer using the Layer Property inspector, select the layer to open the Layer Property inspector. If the Layer Property inspector does not show, open it by choosing Window⇨Properties from the Menu bar. Enter a new name for the layer in the Layer ID field of the Layer Property inspector. Use only alphanumeric characters and avoid special characters including spaces, hyphens, slashes, and periods when naming a layer.

To name a layer by using the Layers panel:

1. Select the layer to open the Layers panel. If the Layers panel does not show, open it by choosing Window⇨Layers from the Menu bar.

2. Double-click the Name column for the layer whose name you want to change. The current name is selected.

3. Enter a new name for the layer.

Dreamweaver updates the associated code for the layer name in the HTML source code for your page.

TIP Try to get in the habit of giving your layers an appropriate name as soon as you create them. The name *blueprint image map* helps you remember a layer's content much better than does the name *Layer 15*.

Nesting Layers

A *nested* layer is a layer that has a dependent relationship with another layer. The nested layer is often referred to as a *child* layer, while the layer on which it depends is called the *parent* layer. A child layer can be drawn completely inside its parent, in an intersecting arrangement with its parent or completely unattached to its parent. A nested layer possesses or *inherits* the same visibility of its parent and moves with the parent when the parent layer is repositioned in the Document window.

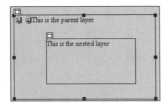

Enabling nesting

To create nested layers in the Document window, you must first enable nesting. To do so, follow these steps:

1. Choose Edit⇨Preferences to open the Preferences dialog box.

2. At the Preferences dialog box, choose Layers in the category area.

3. Check the Nesting check box.

4. Click OK to close the Preferences dialog box.

5. In the Document window, choose Window⇨Layers to open the Layers panel.

6. In the Layers panel, make sure that the Prevent Overlaps box is unchecked.

Creating a new nested layer

Use any of these methods to draw a nested layer:

✔ Click inside an existing layer and choose Insert⇨Layer from the Menu bar. A child layer of default size appears inside the parent layer. (**See also** Part XIII for details on setting layer defaults.) If the dimensions of the parent layer are less than the dimensions of the child layer, the child layer will exceed the boundaries of the parent.

 ✔ Click the Draw Layer button from the Common Objects panel and drag it into the parent layer. A child layer of default size appears inside the parent layer. (**See also** Part XIII for details on setting layer defaults.) If the dimensions of the parent layer are less than the dimensions of the child layer, the child layer will exceed the boundaries of the parent.

✔ Here's a quick way to draw a nested layer and set its dimensions: Click the Draw Layer button from the Common Objects panel. Click the crosshair cursor anywhere in an existing layer and drag until the child layer obtains the dimensions you want relative to the parent layer.

Dreamweaver draws the new child layer and adds the associated code for the new nested layer in the HTML source code for your page.

Changing the nesting of an existing layer

To change the nesting of an existing layer, follow these steps:

1. Open the Layers panel by choosing Window⇨Layers from the Menu bar.

2. In the Layers panel, press and hold the Ctrl key (Windows) or ⌘ key (Macintosh) while using the mouse to click and drag the intended child layer on top of its new parent. The child is in the correct position when you see a box appear around its intended parent layer.

3. Release the mouse button. The new child-parent relationship is shown in the Layers panel.

Dreamweaver draws the new child layer and updates the associated code for changed layer nesting in the HTML source code for your page.

Collapsing or expanding your view in the Layers panel

You can change how you view the names of nested layers in the Layers panel by collapsing or expanding your view.

✔ **To collapse your view:** Click the minus sign (-) in front of a parent layer. Names of nested child layers for that parent are hidden.

✔ **To expand your view:** Click the plus sign (+) in front of a parent layer. Names of nested child layers for that parent show.

Overlapping Layers

Enabling or preventing layer overlap affects where you can draw and position layers in the Document window. Selecting between these two options also impacts how your resulting page appears in various Web browsers.

You may want to prevent layer overlap when working in the Document window because the resulting page may not display properly in some browsers. Or you may want to prevent layer overlap because the Convert Layers to Tables function cannot be executed on overlapping layers.

Alternatively, you may want to enable layer overlap because it provides you greater flexibility in creating your page layout — a page you intend to be viewed primarily through newer browsers.

✔ **To prevent layer overlap:** Open the Layers panel by choosing Window➪Layers from the Menu bar and then checking the Prevent Overlaps check box.

✔ **To enable layer overlap:** Open the Layers panel by choosing Window➪Layers from the Menu bar and making sure that the Prevent Overlaps check box is unchecked.

Placing Objects in a Layer

Dreamweaver adds objects, such as text and images, wherever the blinking insertion point is located. To add an object to a layer, simply click inside the layer and follow the normal procedure for adding the object. For example, add text to a layer by clicking inside the layer and then typing text. Dreamweaver adds the object and updates the associated code for the changed layer in the HTML source code for your page.

Resizing a Layer

Resizing a layer means changing its height and width dimensions. To resize a layer, select the layer and then perform one of the following tasks:

✔ Click and drag a selection handle — one of the large dots on the layer boundary — until the layer obtains the dimensions you desire.

✔ In the Layer Property inspector, enter a new width in pixels at the W box and enter a new length in pixels at the L box. If the Layer Property inspector does not show, open it by choosing Window➪Properties from the Menu bar.

Dreamweaver updates the associated code for the layer's dimensions in the HTML source code for your page.

Resizing multiple layers at the same time

You can change the height and width dimensions of multiple layers at the same time as follows:

1. Press and hold the Shift key while selecting each layer you want to resize.

2. If the Multiple Layers Property inspector does not appear, open it by choosing Window⇨Properties from the Menu bar.

3. In the Multiple Layers Property inspector, enter a new width in pixels at the W box and enter a new length in pixels at the L box.

Dreamweaver updates the associated code for all selected layers' dimensions in the HTML source code for your page.

Selecting a Layer

Selecting a layer enables you to identify which layer you want to affect when executing a layer operation such as moving or naming the layer.

Use any of the following methods to select a layer:

✔ In the Document window, click on the boundary of the layer.

✔ In the Document window, click on the layer handle — the square enclosing a small grid that's located at the top-left corner of the layer.

✔ In the Document window, click on the layer marker that appears as the letter *C* or *N* in a yellow box.

✔ In the Layers panel, click on the name of the layer.

✔ Click on the layer's HTML tag in the tag selector of the Document window status bar.

Selection handles appear on the boundary of the layer to indicate that you have selected it.

Tagging a Layer

Dreamweaver offers you four different HTML tags for labeling layers: `<div>`, `<span>`, `<layer>`, and `<ilayer>`. Each tag has different properties and causes the layer to appear differently on your resulting Web page.

HTML Layer Tag	Cascading Style Sheet or Netscape	Positioning
DIV	CSS	Absolute
SPAN	CSS	Relative
LAYER	Netscape	Absolute or Relative
ILAYER	Netscape	Absolute or Relative

CSS layers can be displayed in both Internet Explorer and Netscape Navigator. Netscape Layers are intended only for display in Netscape Navigator.

Absolutely positioned layers are drawn identically in Web browsers according to specific coordinates you set. Relatively positioned layers are drawn relative to other layers (for instance, parent layers) and may appear differently depending on the setup of each user's browser.

To tag a layer in the Layer Property inspector: Select the layer and then choose a tag from the Tag drop-down list in the Layer Property inspector. Tag choices consist of DIV, SPAN LAYER, and ILAYER. If the Layer Property inspector does not appear, open it by selecting Window➪Properties from the Menu bar. Dreamweaver updates the associated code for the layer tag in the HTML source code for your page.

Be aware that <layer> and <ilayer> are Netscape's proprietary tags and are not supported by the Internet Explorer browser.

Part III

Constructing Pages with Tables

In Dreamweaver, you use tables as more than just functional tools for neatly listing pieces of text information. Tables can be a Web page designer's best friend when it comes to laying out all sorts of page elements from text to images to forms.

In this part . . .

Adding Tables and Table Elements

You can add a table to your Document window by using either the Standard View or the Layout View. (*See also* "The Big Picture: Dreamweaver 4" for details on working with Dreamweaver views.)

To add a table in Standard View:

1. Click the Standard View button in the View region of the Common Objects panel (*Note:* If the Common Objects panel is not visible, choose Window⇨Objects from the Menu bar.)

2. Choose Insert⇨Table from the Menu bar. Alternatively, you can click the Draw Table button on the Common Objects panel.

3. In the Insert Table dialog box, supply the information for each of the following table attributes:

    *   **Rows:** Enter a number in the text box for the number of rows in the table.

    *   **Columns:** Enter a number in the text box for the number of columns in the table.

    *   **Cell Padding:** Enter a number in the text box specifying how many pixels of padding you want between the inside edge of a cell and its contents.

    *   **Cell Spacing:** Enter a number in the text box specifying how many pixels of separation you want between cells.

    *   **Width:** Select Percent from the drop-down list and then enter a number (0 – 100) in the text box for the percent of page width you want the entire table to occupy. Or select Pixels from the drop-down list and enter a number of pixels for the width of the entire table.

    *   **Border:** Enter a number in the text box for the width of the table borders in pixels. Entering 0 causes the borders to disappear.

4. Click OK to accept your selections and close the dialog box.

To add a table in Layout View:

1. Click the Layout View button in the View region of the Common Objects panel.

    Dreamweaver adds the table to the page and creates the associated HTML code.

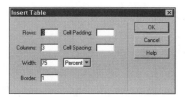

(*Note:* If the Common Objects panel is not visible, choose Window⇨Objects from the Menu bar.)

2. Click the Layout Table button in the Layout region of the Objects panel. Your cursor becomes a crosshair cursor in the Document window.

3. Click in the Document window and drag your mouse to create a table of the dimensions you desire.

Your table appears with a Layout Table tab in the upper-left corner. The table width, in pixels, appears at the top of the table. The Layout Table Property inspector appears and shows the width and height of your new table.

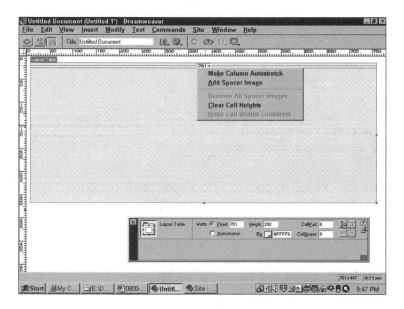

(*Note:* If the Property inspector does not show, open it by choosing Window⇨Properties from the Menu bar.)

Dreamweaver adds the associated code for the table in your HTML page code.

In Layout View, you can click and drag a selection handle on a table to quickly resize the table width and height.

In Layout View, clicking a number that indicates table width or column width opens a pop-up menu where you can make additional formatting changes to your table.

Adding cells to a table

You can add cells to a table either by drawing new cells in Layout View or by splitting existing cells in Standard View. (*See also* "Splitting Cells" later in this part.) To draw a new table cell in Layout View, follow these steps:

1. Click the Layout View button in the View region of the Objects panel.

(*Note:* If the Objects panel is not visible, choose Window⇨Objects from the Menu bar.)

2. Click the Draw Layout Cell button in the Layout region of the Objects panel. Your cursor becomes a crosshair cursor in the table.

3. Click anywhere in the table and drag your mouse to create a cell of the dimensions you desire; then release the mouse button.

Your cell appears in the table, and Dreamweaver adds the associated code for the table cell in your HTML page code.

Create multiple cells in succession by holding down the Ctrl button (Windows) or Cmd button (Macintosh) as you draw each cell.

Adding rows or columns to a table

You can add rows or columns anywhere in an existing table from the Standard View or the Layout View.

To add rows or columns in Standard View:

1. Click the Standard View button in the View region of the Common Objects panel. (*Note:* If the Common Objects panel is not visible, choose Window⇨Objects from the Menu bar.)

2. Click in the table to position the cursor where you want to add rows or columns.

3. Choose Modify⇨Table⇨Insert Rows or Columns from the Menu bar. Alternatively, you can right-click (Windows) or Shift-click (Macintosh) the table and choose Table⇨Insert Rows or Columns from the pop-up menu that appears. Doing so opens the Insert Rows or Columns dialog box.

4. In the Insert Rows or Columns dialog box, click a radio button to indicate whether you want to add Rows or Columns.

5. In the Number of . . . text box, enter a number or click the up or down arrow to indicate the number of rows or columns you want to insert.

6. In the Where area of the dialog box, select where you want to insert the rows or columns.

   • **If you are inserting rows:** Click a radio button to insert the rows Above the Selection or Below the Selection.

   • **If you are inserting columns:** Click a radio button to insert the columns Before the Selection or After the Selection.

7. Click OK to apply your selections and close the dialog box.

To add rows or columns in Layout View:

Follow the same procedure for adding a cell to a table in Layout View (*see also* "Adding Cells to a Table"), but stretch the cell the entire table width to make a row or the entire table height to make a column. You cannot draw over the boundaries of existing rows or columns.

Dreamweaver updates your table and adds the associated code to your HTML page code.

Aligning a Table on a Page

You can align a table in the Document window so that the table is positioned left, center, or right when it's displayed in the Web browser.

✔ **To align a table in Standard View:** Select the table you want to align (*see also* "Selecting a Table" later in this part) and choose an alignment from the <u>A</u>lign drop-down list in the Table Properties inspector that appears. (*Note:* If the Properties inspector does not appear, open it by choosing <u>W</u>indow⇨ <u>P</u>roperties from the Menu bar.) The Default alignment option causes the table to align according to user preferences.

✔ **To align a table in Layout View:** Select the table you want to align (*see also* "Selecting a Table" later in this part). Right-click the mouse and choose Align⇨<u>L</u>eft, <u>C</u>enter, or <u>R</u>ight from the pop-up menu that appears.

Dreamweaver adds the associated code for the table alignment to your HTML page code.

Aligning Information in Table Cells

You can align information in table cells left, center, or right, and you can do so in either Standard or Layout View.

✔ **To align cell contents in Standard View:** Select the cell or cells you want to set alignment for (*see also* "Selecting a Cell" later in this part) and click an alignment button in the Property inspector that appears.

✔ **To align cell contents in Layout View:** Click inside the cell you want to set alignment for (*see also* "Selecting a Cell" later in this part) — without selecting the cell itself — and click an alignment button in the Cell Property inspector that appears.

Dreamweaver adds the associated code for the table alignment to your HTML page code.

If a Property inspector does not appear, open it by choosing <u>W</u>indow⇨<u>P</u>roperties from the Menu bar.

Coloring a Cell Border

You can change the color of any cell border as follows:

1. Click the Standard View button in the View region of the Objects panel. (*Note:* If the Objects panel is not visible, choose <u>W</u>indow⇨<u>O</u>bjects from the Menu bar.)

2. Select the cell (*see also* "Selecting a Cell" later in this part) where you want to change the border color. If the Cell Property inspector does not appear, open it by choosing Window⇨Properties from the Menu bar.

3. In the Cell Property inspector, select a new color from the Brdr color swatch. Alternatively, you can enter a hexadecimal color code into the empty color box.

The cell border changes to the color you select, and Dreamweaver adds the associated code to the HTML code for the page.

Coloring a Table Border

You can change the color of any table border as follows:

1. In Standard View, select the table (*see also* "Selecting a Table" later in this part) where you want to change the border color.

Doing so opens the Table Property inspector. If the Table Property inspector does not show, open it by choosing Window⇨Properties from the Menu bar.

2. In the Table Property inspector, select a new color from the Brdr color swatch. Alternatively, you can enter a hexadecimal color code in the empty color box.

The table border changes to the color you select, and Dreamweaver adds the associated code to the HTML code for the page.

Deleting Tables and Table Elements

To delete a table from a page, select the table (*see also* "Selecting a Table" later in this part) in any view and then press the Backspace or Delete key. Dreamweaver removes the table from your page and deletes the associated code in the HTML for the page.

Deleting a layout cell

To delete a layout cell from a table, select the layout cell in Layout View (*see also* "Selecting a Cell" later in this part) and then press the Backspace or Delete key. Dreamweaver removes the cell from your page and deletes the associated code in the HTML for the page.

Deleting a row or column

Delete a row or column from a table in Standard View as follows:

✔ **To delete a row from a table:** Select the row (**see also** "Selecting a Row or Column" later in this part) and then choose Modify⟹Table⟹Delete Row from the Menu bar.

✔ **To delete a column from a table:** Select the column (**see also** "Selecting a Row or Column" later in this part) and then choose Modify⟹Table⟹Delete Column from the Menu bar.

Dreamweaver removes the row or column from your page and deletes the associated code in the HTML for the page.

You can use the same procedure to delete multiple rows or columns — just be sure to select all the rows or columns you want to delete before you open the Modify menu.

Including a Background Image or Color in a Table

By default, a table possesses the same color or background image as the Document window or layer in which it is drawn. You can change the background of any table by adding a background image or background color to the table. Follow these steps:

1. Click the Standard View button in the View region of the Objects panel. (*Note:* If the Objects panel is not visible, choose Window⟹Objects from the Menu bar.)

2. Select the table (**see also** "Selecting a Table" later in this part) where you want to change the background.

Doing so opens the Table Property inspector. If the Table Property inspector does not appear, open it by choosing Window⟹Properties from the Menu bar.

3. In the Table Property inspector, change one of the following:

• **Bg Color:** Click the color swatch and select a color from the color palette that appears. Alternatively, you can enter a hexadecimal color code in the Bg Color box. The new color appears in the background of the selected table.

• **Bg Image:** Click the folder to the right of the box and browse to select a background image from the Select Image Source dialog box that appears. Click the Select button to accept your image choice and close the dialog box. The name of the background image appears in the Bg Image text box, and the image is added to the background of the table.

Dreamweaver adds the associated code for the table background to the HTML source code for your page.

Including a Background Image or Color in Table Cells

By default, a table cell possesses the same color or background image as the Document window or layer in which it is drawn.

You can change the background of any table cell by adding a background image or background color to the cell. Follow these steps:

1. Click the Standard View button in the View region of the Objects panel. (*Note:* If the Objects panel is not visible, choose Window⇨Objects from the Menu bar.)

2. Select the cell (*see also* "Selecting a Cell" later in this part) where you want to change the background. Doing so opens the Table Property inspector. If the Cell Property inspector does not appear, open it by choosing Window⇨Properties from the Menu bar.

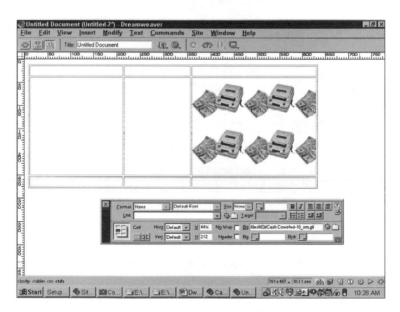

3. At the Cell Property inspector, change one of the following:

- **Bg**: Click the folder to the right of the box and browse to select a background image from the Select Image Source dialog box that appears. Click the Select button to accept your image choice and close the dialog box. The name of the background image appears in the Bg box, and the image is added to the background of the cell.

- **Bg:** Click the color swatch and select a color from the color palette that appears. Alternatively, you can enter a hexadecimal color code in the Bg box. The new color appears in the background of the selected cell.

Dreamweaver adds the associated code for the table cell's background to the HTML source code for your page.

Merging Cells

You can merge two or more cells in Standard View. Select the cells you want to merge (*see also* "Selecting a Cell" later in this part) and use any of the following four procedures:

- ✔ Right-click (Windows) or Shift-click (Macintosh) your selection and then Choose Table⇨Merge Cells from the pop-up menu that appears.

- ✔ Click the Merge Cells button in the Cell Property inspector that appears. (If the Cell Property inspector does not appear, open it by choosing Window⇨Properties from the Menu bar.)

- ✔ Choose Modify⇨Table⇨Merge Cells from the Menu bar.

- ✔ Press Ctrl+Alt+M (Windows).

Your cells merge, and Dreamweaver adds the associated code for the merged cells to the HTML source code for your page.

Naming a Table

If you name a table, you can more easily identify it when you work with the Table Property inspector and when you examine multiple tables in the HTML page code.

To name a table in Standard View, select the table (*see also* "Selecting a Table" later in this part) that you want to name. When you select the table, the Table Property inspector appears. (**Note:** If the Table Property inspector does not appear, open it by choosing Window⇨Properties from the Menu bar.) Enter a new name for the table in the Table Name field of the Table Property inspector. Use only alphanumeric characters and avoid special characters including spaces, hyphens, slashes, and periods.

Dreamweaver updates the associated code for the table name in the HTML source code for your page.

Placing an Object in a Table Cell

Dreamweaver adds objects — such as text and images — at the blinking insertion point.

To add an object to a table cell, switch to Standard View and then click inside the cell and follow the associated procedure for adding the object. (**See also** Part IV for details on adding text and Part V for details on adding images.) Dreamweaver adds the object and updates the associated code for the changed cell in the HTML source code for your page.

Selecting Tables and Table Elements

Selecting a table enables you to work on attributes of the entire table, affecting every cell contained within. You can select a table in either Standard View or Layout View. Use any of the following methods to select a table.

In Standard View:

🗸 Choose Modify⇨Table⇨Select Table from the Menu bar.

🗸 Right-click (Windows) or Ctrl-click (Macintosh) anywhere inside a table to open a pop-up menu where you can choose Table⇨Select Table.

🗸 Click the bottom or right border of the table.

🗸 Move the mouse pointer near the outside edge of the table and click when the cursor becomes a four-arrow compass.

🗸 Select the <table> tag in the Tag Selector area at the bottom of the Document window.

When you select the table, it displays selection handles and a thick, black border.

In Layout View:

- ✔ Click any border of the table.

- ✔ Click the Layout Table tab of the table.

- ✔ Select the `<table>` tag in the Tag Selector area at the bottom of the Document window.

When you select the table, it displays selection handles and a green border.

The green border color of a Layout Table can be changed in the Layout View category of Dreamweaver Preferences (*see also* Part XIII).

Selecting a cell

Selecting a cell enables you to make changes to only that cell. You can select a cell in either Standard View or Layout View. There are several ways of selecting a cell, depending on what you want to edit.

To select a cell:

- ✔ Ctrl+click the cell (Windows) or Cmd+click the cell (Macintosh).

- ✔ Click anywhere inside the cell. (Use this option if you intend to edit cell contents.)

- ✔ In Layout View only, click the cell border to open the Layout Cell Property inspector. (Use this option if you intend to edit other formatting attributes of the cell, such as size.) Your selected cell displays selection handles and a thick, blue border.

The blue border color of a Layout Cell can be changed in the Layout View category of Dreamweaver Preferences (*see also* Part XIII).

Selecting a row or column

Selecting a row or column enables you to work simultaneously on attributes of every cell contained within your selection. Switch to Standard View and then make your selection using any of the following methods.

To select a row:

✔ Move the cursor slightly outside the left border of the row you want to select. When the cursor becomes a thickened arrow, click to select the row.

✔ Click inside the first or last cell in the row you want to select and then drag across the remaining cells in the row.

To select a column:

✔ Move the cursor slightly outside the top border of the column you want to select. When the cursor becomes a thickened arrow, click to select the column.

✔ Click inside the first or last cell in the column you want to select and then drag across the remaining cells in the column.

Cells in your selection display thick, black borders.

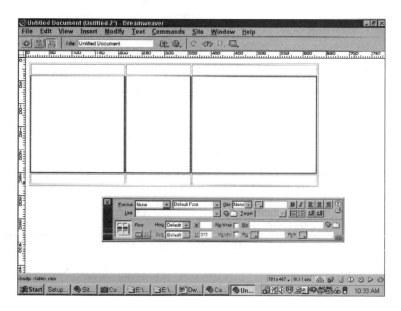

Selecting multiple cells

Selecting multiple cells enables you to make changes affecting only the content and formatting of those cells. Switch to Standard View and then make your selection by holding down the Ctrl key (Windows) or the Cmd key (Macintosh) and clicking on each cell you want to select. Your selected cells display thick, black borders.

Setting Cell Width and Height

You can set the dimensions of a single cell in Layout View. Cell width can be either a fixed width in pixels or a relative — *autostretch* — width that fills a percentage of the entire browser width. Cell height can be set only as a fixed value in pixels. Set cell width and height by using the following procedures.

To set cell width, switch to Layout View and select the cell that you want to adjust. (*See also* "Selecting a Cell" earlier in this part.) When the Layout Cell Property inspector appears, select one of the following options:

✔ **Fixed:** Click the Fixed radio button. In the Layout Cell Property Inspector, enter a width in pixels in the Fixed box. Or drag the right or left cell selection handle until the cell obtains the width you desire. (*Note:* Entering a width in the Property inspector causes the cell to stretch to the right. If the number you enter causes the cell to overlap an existing cell, Dreamweaver informs you that it will stretch a valid value — specifically to a position flush with the cell to the right.)

✔ **Autostretch:** Click the Autostretch radio button. *See also* "Using Autostretch" later in this part.

To set cell height, select the cell (*see also* "Selecting a Cell" earlier in this part) and enter a number in pixels in the Height box. Or drag the top or bottom row boundary until the row obtains the height you desire.

Dreamweaver adds the associated code for the cell width or height to the HTML source code for your page.

Setting the dimensions of a single cell causes all other cells in the same row and column to resize relative to your selection.

Setting Column Width

You can set the width of a column in either Standard View or Layout View. Column width can be either a fixed width in pixels or a relative — *autostretch* — width, which fills a percentage of the entire browser width. Use one of the following procedures to set column width.

 In Standard View: Select the column (***see also*** "Selecting a Column or Row" earlier in this part) and enter a width in pixels or percent at the W box in the Column Property inspector that appears. Or drag the right or left column boundary until the column obtains the width you desire.

 In Layout View: Create either a fixed or autostretch column width as follows:

🖊 **Fixed:** Select a cell (***see also*** "Selecting a Row or Column" earlier in this part) in the column and click the Fixed radio button in the Layout Cell Property Inspector that appears. Enter a width in pixels at the Fixed box or drag the right or left cell selection handle until the column obtains the width you desire. (***Note:*** Entering a width in the Property inspector causes the cell and the associated column to stretch to the right. If the number you enter causes the cell to overlap an existing cell, Dreamweaver informs you that it will stretch a valid value — specifically to a position flush with the cell to the right.)

🖊 **Autostretch:** Click the column width at the top of the column you want to affect and select Make Column Autostretch from the pop-up menu. ***See also*** "Using Autostretch" later in this part.

Dreamweaver adds the associated code for the column width to the HTML source code for your page.

Setting Row Height

 You can set the height of a row in Standard View. Select the row (***see also*** "Selecting a Row or Column" earlier in this part) and enter a height in pixels in the H box of the Row Property inspector that appears. Or drag the top or bottom row boundary until the row obtains the height you desire.

Splitting Cells

You can split a single cell into two or more cells in Standard View as follows:

1. Select the cell (**see also** "Selecting a Cell" earlier in this part) that you want to split.

2. Indicate that you want to split the cell by using any of the four following procedures:

   • Right-click (Windows) or Shift-click (Macintosh) your selection and then select Table➪Split Cell from the pop-up menu that appears.

   • Click the Split Cells button in the Cell Property inspector that appears. If the Cell Property inspector does not appear, open it by choosing Window➪Properties from the Menu bar.

   • Choose Modify➪Table➪Split Cells from the Menu bar.

3. In the Split Cell dialog box that appears, click a radio button to indicate whether you want to split the cell into Rows or Columns.

4. In the Split Cell dialog box, enter a number in the Number of . . . box to indicate how many rows or columns you want to split the cell into. You can click the spinner arrows to increase or decrease your number.

5. Click OK to apply your change and close the dialog box.

Your cell splits, and Dreamweaver adds the associated code to the HTML source code for your page.

Using Autostretch

Autostretch is a new feature in Dreamweaver 4 that enables you to make a table stretch to fill the entire width of a user's browser. Only one column in a table can be set to autostretch. The autostretch feature works by adding a placeholder, or *spacer image,* to the column you designate for stretching. The spacer image is a transparent image that cannot be seen in the browser.

Applying autostretch

You can apply autostretch to any table you want as follows:

1. Click the Layout View button in the View region of the Common Objects panel. If the Common Objects panel is not visible, choose <u>W</u>indow⇨<u>O</u>bjects from the Menu bar.

2. Click the column indicator at the top of the column you want to affect and select Make Column Autostretch from the pop-up menu.

   Alternatively, you can click a cell in the column and click the <u>A</u>utostretch radio button at the Table Cell Property inspector that appears. If the Property inspector does not show, open it by choosing <u>W</u>indow⇨<u>P</u>roperties from the Menu bar.

   Note: The Choose Spacer Image dialog box may appear under certain circumstances. ***See also*** "Choosing a spacer image" earlier in this part.

The column indicator changes to show that the column is set to autostretch.

Column indicators   Autostretch indicator

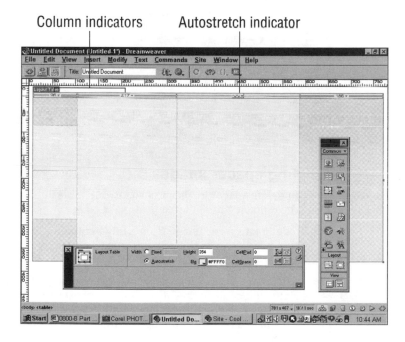

Choosing a spacer image

The first time you use the autostretch feature, a Choose Spacer Image dialog box appears. If you set a spacer image for the site in the Layout View category of Dreamweaver Preferences (*see also* Part XIII), the dialog box does not appear.

At the Choose Autostretch Image dialog box, click a radio button for one of these options:

🖊 **Create a spacer image file.** This option opens a dialog box where you can save the spacer image file. Be sure to save the spacer image file in the site root where your document with the table is saved.

🖊 **Use an existing spacer image file.** Choose this option to locate an existing spacer image file you have saved for your site.

🖊 **Don't use spacer images for autostretch tables.** Choosing this option causes columns in your table to collapse to the width of the content that they contain. This option may cause your table, when viewed in a browser, to appear markedly different from your Layout Table.

Click OK to apply your selection and close the dialog box.

Deleting spacer images

You can delete spacer images from a Layout Table in Layout View using the following procedures.

🖊 **To delete a spacer image from a table column:** Click the column indicator of the column and select Remove Spacer Image from the pop-up menu.

🖊 **To delete all spacer images from a Layout Table:** Click any column indicator of the Layout Table and select Remove All Spacer Images from the pop-up menu. Alternatively, you can click the Remove Spacer Image button in the Layout Table Property inspector. (*Note:* If the Property inspector does not show, open it by choosing Window⊅Properties from the Menu bar.)

Wrapping Cell Contents

Content contained in a cell normally wraps to the next line when it exceeds the cell width. You can instead turn on the No Wrap option so that the cell stretches in width as you type, keeping your text all on a single line. You can toggle between wrapping and not wrapping by using the No Wrap option as follows:

✔ **In Standard View:** Select the cell so that the Cell Property Inspector appears (*see also* "Selecting a Cell" earlier in this part). Leave the check box unchecked to activate wrapping. Click the N<u>o</u> Wrap check box to turn content wrapping off.

✔ **In Layout View:** Select the cell so that the Layout Cell Property Inspector appears (*see also* "Selecting a Cell" earlier in this part). Leave the check box unchecked to activate wrapping. Click the N<u>o</u> Wrap check box to turn content wrapping off.

Part IV

Putting Words on a Page

The vast majority of content displayed on the Web takes the form of text. Adding text to a page is similar to typing text in a word processing document. You can format font, size, color, and attributes, such as bold and italics. You can also create special characters — such as the copyright symbol or quotes — as well as special formatting, such as bulleted or numbered lists. Finally, you can manage more advanced text formatting by using Cascading Style Sheets (CSS).

In this part . . .

Adding Text

You can add text directly to the Document window, in a layer, or in a table cell. To add text, simply click your cursor anywhere on your page and begin typing. The Text Property inspector appears so that you can format your new text. If the inspector doesn't appear, open it by choosing <u>W</u>indow⇨<u>P</u>roperties from the Menu bar. Click the expander arrow to see all options in the inspector.

Alignment buttons

Format menu

Font menu   Italic

Size menu   Bold

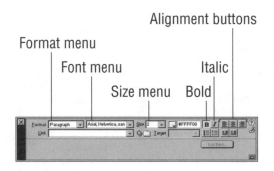

 To save time in editing the text you add, set as defaults the HTML text attributes you most frequently use. To do so, choose <u>E</u>dit⇨Preference<u>s</u> to open the Preferences dialog box. Then choose Fonts/Encoding from the Category menu and make selections for your Dreamweaver text defaults.

Aligning Text

You can align text left, center, or right. To do so, select the paragraph of text you want to align. Then click an Alignment button in the Text Property inspector. (If the inspector doesn't appear, open it by choosing <u>W</u>indow⇨<u>P</u>roperties from the Menu bar.) Alternatively, you can choose <u>T</u>ext⇨<u>A</u>lign from the Menu bar and choose either <u>L</u>eft, <u>C</u>enter, or <u>R</u>ight from the pop-up menu.

Breaking Text with Line Breaks

Including line breaks when typing text in the Dreamweaver Document window is a slightly different process than including line breaks in a word processing program. In HTML, pressing Enter (Windows) or Return (Macintosh) creates a paragraph break — not a line break. To manipulate line breaks, use the following procedures.

Inserting a line break

 To insert a line break on a page, choose Insert⇨Line Break from the Menu bar or press Shift+Enter (Windows) or Shift+Return (Macintosh). Alternatively, you may select the Insert Line Break button from the Characters Objects panel. (If the panel does not show, open it by choosing Window⇨Objects from the Menu bar.) Dreamweaver places the cursor at the start of the next line and creates the line break HTML code for the page.

Deleting a line break

To delete a break from a page, place the cursor at the beginning of the line immediately following the line break and press the Backspace key. Dreamweaver removes the break from your page and deletes the associated code in the HTML for the page.

Coloring Text

To add color to your text, select the text you want to color. Then click the color swatch in the Text Property inspector and select a color from the color palette. Or, you can enter a hexadecimal color code, such as #FFFFFF for white, in the color box. (If the inspector doesn't appear, open it by choosing Window⇨Properties from the Menu bar.) Alternatively, you can choose Text⇨Color from the Menu bar and make a choice at the Color dialog box.

 Want to select from color choices other than the Web Safe panel? Click the Expander button in any color palette and click to deselect the Snap to Web Safe option. But be aware that non-Web safe colors do not appear identically on Macintosh and Windows systems.

Formatting Text

Text formatted according to traditional HTML standards displays in a user's browser according to a hierarchical standard. You can select paragraph or heading formats, with headings bolded and ranging in size from Heading 1, the largest, to Heading 6, the smallest. These formats don't correspond to an exact size in the user's browser; the only guarantee is that Heading 1 is the largest heading, Heading 6 is the smallest, and paragraph text is presented in a proportional, unbolded style. The exact formatting of text depends on settings in the user's browser. For example, in Internet Explorer, the actual size of text depends on whether the text size is set at Smallest, Small, Medium, Large, or Largest.

To format text, select the text you want to format and then choose a format from the Format drop-down menu in the Text Property inspector. (If the inspector doesn't show, open it by choosing Window⇨Properties from the Menu bar.) Choices consist of None, Paragraph, Heading 1 through Heading 6, and Preformatted. (**See also** "Using HTML Text Styles" later in this part for details on working with preformatted text.) Alternatively, you can choose Text⇨Paragraph Format from the Menu bar and choose a formatting option from the drop-down menu.

Indenting and Outdenting Text

To indent text: Select the text you want to affect and click the Indent button in the Text Property inspector. (If the inspector doesn't appear, open it by choosing Window⇨Properties from the Menu bar.) Alternatively, you can choose Text⇨Indent from the Menu bar.

To outdent text: Select the text you want to affect and click the Outdent button in the Text Property inspector. Alternatively, you can choose Text⇨Outdent from the Menu bar.

Listing Text

If you want to create lists of text items, use the following procedure:

1. In either the Document window, in a layer, or in a table cell, select one or more list items in your text.

2. In the Text Property inspector, click one of the List buttons. Your options consist of the Unordered List button and the Ordered List button. (If the inspector doesn't appear, open it by choosing Window⇨Properties from the Menu bar.)

3. In the Text Property inspector, click the List Item button to open the List Properties dialog box.

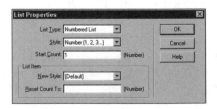

4. In the List Properties dialog box, make selections for the following items:

- **List Type:** Options on the drop-down menu consist of Bulleted, Numbered, Directory, or Menu.

- **Style:** Available when you select Bulleted or Numbered list types. For the Bulleted list type, options on the drop-down menu consist of Bullet or Square. For the Numbered list type, options consist of Number (1, 2, 3...), Roman Small (i, ii, iii...), Roman Large (I, II, III...), Alphabet Small (a, b, c...), and Alphabet Large (A, B, C...).

- **Start Count:** Available only when you select the Numbered list type. Enter the number you want the current list to start at.

- **New Style:** Available when you select Bulleted or Numbered list types. You can choose from the drop-down menu a new style for the currently selected list items. The new style is applied only to the current selection, not to the entire list.

- **Reset Count To:** Available only when you select the Numbered list type. Enter the number you want the selected list item to be presented in the list. If you have selected more than one list item, type the number where you want the selection to start.

5. Click OK.

The List Properties dialog box closes, and your changes are applied. The HMTL page code is updated to include your changes.

 You can also create and edit text lists using menu commands by choosing Text➪List from the Menu bar.

Selecting Text Fonts

When adding text to a page, you can select any text font you want — but your safest bet is to use fonts that are standard on most users' systems. Otherwise, you run the risk of having users' systems replace your font and display the closest available resident font.

Applying a font

To apply a font to your text, follow this procedure:

1. Select the text you want where you want to apply a font. Doing so opens the Text Property inspector. (If the inspector doesn't appear, open it by choosing Window➪Properties from the Menu bar.)

2. In the Text Property inspector, choose a font from the Font drop-down menu. Alternatively, you can choose Text⇨Font from the Menu bar.

Dreamweaver applies your font selection and updates the HTML page code. When displaying your page, a user's browser shows your text using the first font in the font list that is available on the user's computer.

Editing the font menu

You can add new fonts to the Font menu in the Text Property inspector as follows:

1. In the Text Property inspector, select Edit Font List from the Font drop-down menu. Doing so opens the Edit Font List dialog box.

2. In the Edit Font List dialog box, click a font in the Available Fonts category.

3. Click the left-pointing double arrow button to move your selected font to the Chosen Fonts list. To remove a font from the Chosen Fonts list, click the right-pointing double arrow button.

4. Repeat Steps 2 and 3 to add new fonts in sequence to your new listing.

5. Click the Add (+) button to add your group of Chosen Fonts to the Font List.

6. Remove any listing in the Font List by first clicking the listing and then clicking the Remove (-) button.

7. Resequence the Font List by first clicking any listing and then clicking the up-or down-arrow buttons to move its position in the list. Doing so enables you to place your most-used selections conveniently at the top of the Font List.

8. Click OK to accept your selections and close the dialog box.

Sans-serif fonts typically display on-screen with greater readability than serif fonts.

Setting Text Styles

Set text styles using the following procedure:

1. Select the text you want to affect.

2. Choose Text⇨Style from the Menu bar and select a style from the drop-down menu.

   Options consist of: Bold, Italics, Underline, Strikethrough, Teletype, Emphasis, Strong, Code, Variable, Sample, Keyboard, Citation, and Definition.

Dreamweaver applies your style and adds the associated HTML to your page code.

 You can bold or italicize text quickly by selecting text and then clicking the associated button at the Text Property Inspector. (If the inspector doesn't appear, open it by choosing Window⇨Properties from the Menu bar.)

Sizing Text

You can assign either a general font size or a relative font size for your text. General font sizes range from 1 to 7 — 1 is the smallest font size, and 7 is the largest. Relative font sizes range from –7 to +7, relative to the base font size. These sizes do not correspond to specific point sizes and appear differently depending on a user's browser settings. The default base font size is 3, but you can change the size in Dreamweaver Preferences. (To do so, choose Edit⇨Preferences from the Menu bar and then choose the Fonts/Encoding category where you can make your changes.)

To size text, select the text you want to format and then choose a format from the Size drop-down menu in the Text Property inspector. (If the Inspector doesn't appear, open it by choosing Window⇨Properties from the Menu bar.) The None choice is the default setting.

Alternatively, you can choose Text⇨Size from the Menu bar and chooset a general font size from the drop-down menu. Or you can choose Text⇨Size Change from the Menu bar and select a relative font size from the drop-down menu.

Spell Checking Text

Nothing ruins an elegantly assembled Web site faster than spelling errors. Fortunately, Dreamweaver can help troubleshoot potential misspellings by offering you a spell-checking function. You can spell check a selection of text or an entire document.

To run the spell checker, follow these steps:

1. Select the text you want to check or select nothing to check the entire page.

2. Choose Text⇨Check Spelling from the Menu bar.

3. In the Check Spelling dialog box, unrecognized words are listed one at a time in the Word Not Found in Dictionary box. When a word turns up as unrecognized, perform one of these actions:

   • **Skip over the word:** Click the Ignore button. To skip over all instances of the flagged word, click Ignore All.

   • **Change the word:** Select a replacement word from the Suggestions list or enter your change in the Change To box; then click Change. To change all instances of the flagged word, click Change All.

   • **Add the word to your personal dictionary:** Click the Add to Personal button to include the flagged word in your personal dictionary. Doing so exempts the word from being flagged in future spell checks.

Dreamweaver makes the changes you designate and updates the HTML page code.

Manage entries in your personal dictionary by using a text editor to edit the `Personal.dat` file located in

`Dreamweaver 4/Configuration/Dictionaries.`

Typing Special Characters

For characters you cannot enter directly on the keyboard (such as the Trademark symbol) or for characters that are reserved for other uses in HTML (such as quotes), Dreamweaver provides an alternative way of creating these special signs.

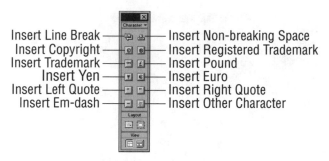

Insert Line Break —— Insert Non-breaking Space
Insert Copyright —— Insert Registered Trademark
Insert Trademark —— Insert Pound
Insert Yen —— Insert Euro
Insert Left Quote —— Insert Right Quote
Insert Em-dash —— Insert Other Character

Adding a special text character

Place your cursor at the location where you want to add a special character and then click the appropriate Character button from the options available on the Character Objects panel. (If the Character Objects panel doesn't appear, open it by choosing Window⇨ Objects from the Menu bar.) Dreamweaver adds the character to your document and the associated HTML to your page code.

Using Other Characters

To add a character not shown as a button in the Character Objects panel, including foreign language symbols, follow these steps:

1. Place your cursor at the location where you want to add the character and then click the Other Character button in the Character Objects panel. (If the Character Objects panel doesn't appear, open it by choosing Window⇨Objects from the Menu bar.) The Insert Other Character dialog box appears.

2. In the Insert Other Character dialog box, click the character you want to use. The HTML code for the character shows in the Insert box.

3. Click OK to add the character to your document and close the dialog box.

Dreamweaver adds the associated HTML to your page code.

Using HTML Text Styles

For combinations of text formatting, fonts, sizes, colors, and styles you use repeatedly, you can create and apply HTML text styles. Creating an HTML text style enables you to use a single, aggregate step to replace multiple individual steps in applying text attributes. The HTML text styles are set up in the HTML Styles panel and are applicable only for the current site.

Creating or editing an HTML text style

You can create a new HTML text style or edit an existing style by following these steps:

1. Click the Show HTML Styles icon on either Launcher or choose Window⇨HTML Styles from the Menu bar. Doing so opens the HTML Styles panel for your current site.

2. To create a new style, click the New Style button. To edit an existing style, double-click the style name in the panel. Doing so opens the Define HTML Style dialog box.

3. In the Define HTML Style dialog box, choose the attributes you want to assign to your style. Formatting options include font, color, and size.

4. Click OK to close the dialog box and add (or update) the style in the HTML Styles panel.

Delete an existing HTML text style in the HTML Styles panel by selecting the style and clicking the Delete Style button. Deleting a style does not remove or change the attributes of text already formatted with that style.

Editing an HTML style does not automatically cause text previously formatted with that style to be updated with the edited style.

Applying an HTML text style

Apply an HTML text style to text by using these steps:

1. Select the text you want to affect.

2. If the HTML Styles panel does not already show, open it by clicking the Show HTML Styles icon on either Launcher or by choosing Window⇔HTML Styles from the Menu bar.

3. In the HTML Styles panel, select the HTML style you want to use and then click the Apply button. To automatically apply the style without clicking Apply each time, select the check box next to the Apply button.

Dreamweaver makes the changes you designate and updates the HTML page code.

Manual HTML formatting that you apply after formatting text with HTML Styles takes precedence.

Working with CSS Text Styles

Cascading Style Sheets (CSS) provide you with the power to format your pages in such a way that users' browsers cannot modify your exact specifications. You can modify text formatting, fonts, sizes, colors, and styles — as well as numerous other page attributes, including positioning and backgrounds.

CSS styles can also save you a great deal of time. After you create a style, you can use a single, aggregate step to replace multiple individual steps in applying the formatting. Additionally, you can make your CSS styles applicable to only the current page or to multiple pages — even an entire site — by creating an external style sheet.

Like HTML styles, changes you make to a defined CSS style are automatically applied to all instances of that style throughout your affected pages and sites — a real time-saver.

Creating a CSS text style

To create a new CSS text style or edit an existing style, follow these steps:

1. Click the Show CSS Styles icon on either Launcher or choose Window⇨CSS Styles from the Menu bar. Doing so opens the CSS Styles panel for your current site.

2. Click the New Style button. Clicking this button opens the New Style dialog box.

3. In the New Style dialog box, enter a name for your style or choose a name from the Name drop-down list.

4. In the Type area of the New Style dialog box, click the Make Custom Style (class) radio button.

5. In the Define In area of the New Style dialog box, select a radio button for where the CSS style resides. Options consist of:

   • **Drop-down list of style sheets:** Choose New Style Sheet File to create a new style sheet or choose an existing sheet from the list. *Note:* If you select New Style Sheet File, a Save Style Sheet File dialog box appears. Enter a file name and browse to the location where you want to save the style sheet. Then click Save.

   • **This Document Only:** The style exists only in the current document.

6. Click OK to close the New Style dialog box and open the Style Definition dialog box.

7. In the Style Definition dialog box, choose Type from the Category list.

8. In the Style Definition dialog box, select the formatting you want to assign to your CSS style. Formatting options include font, color, and size.

9. Click OK to close the dialog box and add the style to the CSS Styles panel.

When formatting CSS text, use pixels — not points — to ensure that users cannot resize your text.

Only 4.0 and later versions of Netscape Navigator and Internet Explorer browsers support CSS styles.

Manual HTML formatting that you apply after formatting text with CSS styles takes precedence.

Editing a CSS text style

You can edit an existing CSS text style by following these steps:

1. If the CSS Styles panel does not already show, open it by clicking the Show CSS Styles icon on either Launcher or by choosing Window➪CSS Styles from the Menu bar.

2. Double-click the style name in the panel. Doing so opens the Style Definition dialog box.

3. In the Style Definition dialog box, edit the formatting of your style.

4. Click OK to close the dialog box and update the style in the CSS Styles panel.

All text formatted with CSS styles is updated to include your edits.

Applying a CSS text style

Apply a CSS text style to text using these steps:

1. Select the text you want to affect.

2. If the CSS Styles panel does not already show, open it by clicking the Show CSS Styles icon on either launcher or choosing Window➪CSS Styles from the Menu bar.

3. In the CSS Styles panel, choose the CSS style you want to use and click the Apply button. To automatically apply the style without clicking Apply each time, select the check box next to the Apply button.

Dreamweaver makes the changes you designate and updates the HTML page code.

Attaching a CSS Style Sheet

Attaching a CSS Style Sheet to a page enables you to apply styles defined in that external sheet to the current document. This feature makes styles that you commonly use transportable between documents and sites. CSS Style Sheets use .css as their file extension.

Attach a CSS Style Sheet as follows:

1. If the CSS Styles panel does not already show, open it by clicking the CSS Styles icon on either Launcher or by choosing Window⇨CSS Styles from the Menu bar.

2. In the CSS Styles panel, click the Attach Style Sheet button. A Select Style Sheet File dialog box appears.

3. Browse to the location of the style sheet you want to use.

4. Click Select to attach the style sheet.

Editing a CSS Style Sheet

To edit an existing CSS Style Sheet, follow these steps:

1. If the CSS Styles panel does not already show, open it by clicking the CSS Styles icon on either Launcher, or by choosing Window⇨CSS Styles from the Menu bar.

2. In the CSS Styles panel, click the Edit Style Sheet button.

An Edit Style Sheet dialog box appears.

3. In the Edit Style Sheet dialog box, select the style sheet you want to edit.

4. Click Edit to open the Style Definition dialog box where you can edit the sheet. After making your edits, click Save to save your style sheet and return to the Edit Style Sheet dialog box. You can also remove any style sheet by clicking the Remove button in the Edit Style Sheet dialog box.

5. Click Done to close the Edit Style Sheet dialog box.

Part V

Working with Images

Images are the key to making your Web site look colorful, eye-catching, and informative. Images include everything from photographs to cartoons, and they create whatever aesthetic feel you want to convey to the user — bold and powerful, playful and sassy, authoritative and reserved, or even hip and funky. Be aware, however, that while images add appeal, they can also increase the download time for users accessing your site. Using a balanced approach to blending images with text and other elements can keep your site both exciting and manageable.

In this part . . .

Adding an Image

You can add an image anywhere you want on a Web page — in a table cell, in a layer, or directly to the Document window itself.

To add an image:

1. Click to position the cursor where you want to add the image.

2. Choose Insert⇔Image from the Menu bar. Alternatively, you may select the Insert Image button from the Common Objects panel. If the Common Objects panel doesn't show, open it by choosing Window⇔Objects from the Menu bar.

3. At the Select Image Source dialog box, click the image you want to insert. If the image is outside the current folder, click the arrow tab beside the Look In box and browse to select the file you want.

4. Click the Select button to insert the image.

If you attempt to insert an image from outside the root folder containing the current site, Dreamweaver asks whether you want to copy the image to the current site root folder. Click Yes. In the Copy File As dialog box, you can enter a new name for the image in the File Name box, or you can accept the current name and click Save.

Dreamweaver places the image on your page and creates a reference to the file in the HTML code for the page.

Adding an Image Border

Adding a border to an image creates a rectangular frame around the image. You can choose whatever thickness you want. Create an image border as follows:

1. Click the image in the Document window to select it. The Image Property inspector appears. If the inspector does not appear, open it by choosing Window⇔Properties from the Menu bar.

2. In the Image Property inspector, click the expander arrow to view the entire inspector. Enter a number in the Border box to add a border of that thickness to the image. Border thickness is measured in pixels.

When your modification is made, Dreamweaver also modifies the associated code in the HTML for the page.

Aligning an Image

You can align images within table cells, within layers, or in the Document window. An image can be aligned left, center, or right. However, you can use numerous other options for wrapping nearby text around an image.

To align an image the quick and easy way: Click the image in the Document window to select it. The Image Property inspector appears. If the inspector does not appear, open it by choosing Window⇨Properties from the Menu bar.

In the Image Property Inspector, click an Alignment button to position the image on the page (or within a cell if the image is located in a table cell). Alignment button choices consist of Left, Center, and Right.

To align an image with special word wrapping: Click the image in the Document window to select it. At the Image Property inspector, choose one of the following alignment options from the Align drop-down list.

Alignment Option	Effect on Image and Text Wrapping
Browser Default	Same as Bottom alignment
Baseline	Same as Bottom alignment
Top	Aligns the image top with the highest other inline element
Middle	Aligns the image middle with the text baseline
Bottom	Aligns the image bottom with the text baseline
Text Top	Aligns the image top with the text top
Absolute Middle	Aligns the image middle with the text middle
Absolute Bottom	Aligns the image bottom with the bottom of the text descenders
Left	Aligns the image flush left
Right	Aligns the image flush right

After you choose an alignment, Dreamweaver modifies the associated code in the HTML for the page.

 The *baseline* of the text is the bottom of the text, ignoring the descenders of letters such as *p* (letters that have segments that fall below the baseline).

Changing an Image Source

After you add an image to a Web page, you may decide to use a different image in its place. You don't have to delete the original image and add a new one — instead, you can change the source of the image. Just follow these steps:

1. Click the image in the Document window to select it. The Image Property inspector appears. If it does not appear, open it by choosing Window⇨Properties from the Menu bar.

2. In the Image Property inspector, click the Src Folder button.

3. In the Select Image Source dialog box, click the image you want to insert. If the image is outside the current folder, click the arrow tab beside the Look In box and browse to select the file you want.

4. Click the Select button to insert the image.

   Note: Every image you want to include on a Web page must reside within the root folder of the current site. If you attempt to insert an image from another location, Dreamweaver asks whether you want to copy the image to the current site root folder. Click Yes. In the Copy File As dialog box, you can enter a new name for the image in the File Name box, or you can accept the current name and click Save.

Dreamweaver places the image on your page and creates a reference to the file in the HTML code for the page.

Choosing an Image Format

Regardless of the software you use to create images for inclusion in your Web pages, you must save images in an HTML-compatible format. Three such formats exist — GIF (Graphics Interchange Format), JPEG (Joint Photographic Experts Group), and PNG (Portable Network Graphics).

Each format possesses attributes that may be advantageous — or not — when constructing your site. Some of these attributes are:

✔ **Maximum Number of Colors:** The more colors, the more realistic the image appears, but the larger the file size and the longer the download time.

✔ **Transparency:** This feature enables you to select a color that becomes transparent when your image is presented in a browser. The advantage is that you can present images with non-rectangular borders.

✔ **Interlace:** An image saved with the interlace feature activated gives the user something to look at as the image downloads — a sort of preview of the image to come.

✔ **Compression:** Compressed images require smaller file sizes and, therefore, download more rapidly. Compression may be *lossless,* meaning no image quality is sacrificed, or *lossy,* meaning some image quality is lost.

The following table compares the attributes of each available image format:

Image Format	Max # Colors	Best for...	Transparency	File Size
GIF	256	Illustrations, logos	yes	small, lossless compression
JPEG	Millions	Photographs	no	depends, lossy compression
PNG	Millions	All images	yes	small, lossless compression

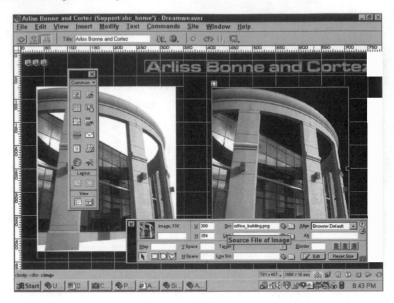

 As a general rule, you want to attempt to minimize the file size of all images you use in the design of your Web pages. Smaller file sizes lead to faster download times and a more user-friendly site.

Deleting an Image

To delete an image from a page, click the image wherever it resides in the Document window and press the Delete key on your keyboard. Dreamweaver removes the image from your page and deletes the associated code in the HTML code for the page.

Editing an Image

Dreamweaver does not enable you to edit images directly, but it does offer an easy way to invoke an image editor so that you can edit an image in your document.

To edit an image, follow these steps:

1. Click the image in the Document window to select it. The Image Property inspector appears. If the inspector does not appear, open it by choosing Window⇔Properties from the Menu bar.

2. In the Image Property inspector, click the Edit button. Doing this starts your image-editing program and opens the image in that program.

3. In your image-editing program, edit the image as you desire.

4. In your image-editing program, save your edited image. The edited image replaces the previous version in your Dreamweaver image files.

The image is updated in your Dreamweaver Document window.

You can set which image-editing program is invoked in Dreamweaver Preferences. Choose Edit⇨Preferences from the Menu bar. In the Preferences dialog box, choose File Types/Editors from the Category menu. Click an image extension (.gif, .jpg, or .png) in the Extensions menu. Then choose a program in the Editors menu and click the Make Primary button. You can add a new Editor by clicking the add (+) button. Click OK to apply your changes and close the dialog box.

Establishing a Low Source Image

A *low source image* is a simplified version of a large file size image (a *high source image*) that you include on a Web page. The low source image is typically a grayscale copy of the main image, and it has a smaller file size and faster download time than the main image. When a user accesses your Web page, the low source image downloads first — giving the user a preview of the more elaborate image to come.

To include a low source image on a page, follow these steps:

1. In your image-editing program, create both the high source and the low source version of your image.

2. In the Document window, add the high source image to your Web page. The high source image is added, and the Image Property inspector appears. If the inspector does not appear, open it by choosing Window⇨Properties from the Menu bar.

3. In the Image Property inspector, click the Low Src Folder button.

4. At the Select Image Source dialog box, click the low source image you want to use. If the image is outside the current folder, click the arrow tab beside the Look In box and browse to select the file you want.

5. Click the Select button to insert the image.

    Note: Every image you want to include on a Web page must reside within the root folder of the current site. If you attempt to insert an image from another location, Dreamweaver asks whether you want to copy the image to the current site root folder. Click Yes. At the Copy File As dialog box, you can enter a new name for the image in the File Name box, or you can accept the current name and click Save.

Dreamweaver includes a reference to the low source image in the HTML code for the page.

Naming an Image

Naming an image enables you to easily identify references to the image in the HTML page code. Providing an image name also enables you to refer to the image in scripting languages such as JavaScript.

To name an image, click the image in the Document window to select it. The Image Property inspector appears. If the inspector does not appear, open it by choosing Window⇨Properties from the Menu bar. In the Image Property inspector, enter a name in the image box next to the thumbnail view of your selected image.

Dreamweaver updates the HTML page code to reflect the name of the image.

Padding an Image

You can pad an image by specifying vertical and horizontal standoff space between the image and any elements surrounding it. Adding vertical space to an image pads the top and bottom of the image, while adding horizontal space to an image pads the left and right sides of the image. Pad an image using the following procedure:

1. Click the image in the Document window to select it. The Image Property inspector appears. If it does not appear, open it by choosing Window⇨Properties from the Menu bar.

2. In the Image Property inspector, enter a number in pixels in the V Space box for the vertical space you want.

3. In the Image Property inspector, enter a number in pixels in the H Space box for the horizontal space you want.

Dreamweaver updates the HTML page code to reflect the padding of the image.

Placing an Image in the Page Background

A simple way to create an image-enhanced Web page that downloads quickly is to add an image to the page background. Just follow these steps:

1. Open the Page Properties dialog box by choosing Modify⇨Page Properties from the Menu bar.

2. In the Background Image area, click the Browse button to open the Select Image Source dialog box.

3. In the Select Image Source dialog box, click the Image you want to insert

   In the image is outside the current folder, click the arrow tab beside the Look In box and browse to select the file you want.

4. Click the Select button to insert the image.

   Note: If you attempt to insert an image from outside the root folder containing the current site, Dreamweaver asks whether you want to copy the image to the current site root folder. Click Yes. At the Copy File As dialog box, you can enter a new name for the image in the File Name box, or you can accept the current name and click Save.

Dreamweaver places the image in the background of your page. If the image is smaller than the background area, Dreamweaver tiles the image (repeats it in checkerboard fashion) to cover the entire area. Dreamweaver also creates a reference to the file in the HTML code for the page.

The image should be a simple square or rectangle shape and consist of a limited-contrast pattern or logo that doesn't interfere with the readability of page text placed in the foreground.

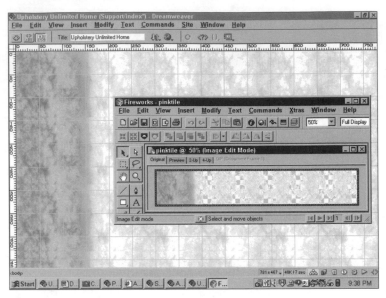

Repositioning an Image

You can reposition an image by moving it to another position within a block of text, moving it from one table cell to another, or even from one layer to another. To reposition an image, simply click the image to select it, drag it to a new location, and release the mouse button. Dreamweaver updates the HTML page code to reflect the new position of the image.

Resizing an Image

Regardless of the original size of an image you want to include on a Web page, Dreamweaver enables you to resize the image to change its dimensions or scale the entire image up or down.

To resize an image, begin by clicking the image in the Document window to select it. The Image Property inspector appears. If the inspector does not appear, open it by choosing Window⊅Properties from the Menu bar. Continue resizing the image by using either of the following methods:

✓ **Click and drag a sizing handle to change the dimensions of the image.** To resize the image maintaining the same proportions, hold down the Shift key while dragging a sizing handle.

✔ **At the Image Property inspector, enter numbers for the exact dimensions of the image.** Enter a number in pixels in the W̲ box for the width of the image and a number in pixels in the H̲ box for the height of the image.

When your modification is made, Dreamweaver also modifies the associated code in the HTML for the page.

To restore a resized image to its original dimensions, click the Reset Image button in the Image Property inspector for the image.

You can enter numbers with other units — such as *in* for inches or *pt* for points — in the W̲ and H̲ boxes of the Image Property inspector. You must include the abbreviation for your selected units.

If you are planning to scale a large image down significantly, it's smarter to perform the resize in your image-editing program, not in the Image Property inspector in Dreamweaver. The reason? Scaling down a large image in Dreamweaver does not actually reduce the file size and, therefore, does not reduce the download time of the image. Save your users some wait time by resizing the image file — not just the way it's presented on-screen.

Showing Alternative Text in Lieu of an Image

Many Internet users choose to speed their Web-surfing activities by disabling automatic downloading of images. Users may choose to view an image only if the text description catches their interest. For these users, you may want to create alternative text for each image you include on your site.

To create Alt text, click the image in the Document window to select it. The Image Property inspector appears. If the inspector does not appear, open it by choosing W̲indow➪P̲roperties from the Menu bar. In the Image Property inspector, enter the alternative text you want to appear for your selected image in the Al̲t box.

Dreamweaver updates the HTML page code to reflect the alternative text for the image.

Visually impaired Web users may benefit from your use of Alt text if they access sites with the help of a speech synthesizer.

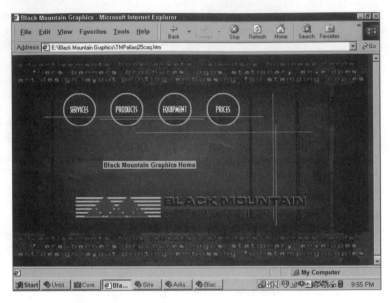

Part VI

Incorporating Interactive Images

Images add content and interest to a Web page. However, if you really want to add pizzazz, you can choose to add not just images, but *interactive* images to your site. Interactive images offer users more than just pretty pictures to look at; some interactive images feature motion, others have *hotspots* that link to other pages, and still others serve as navigation buttons that enable users to move through the site. Interactive images can be added in either Standard View or Layout View.

Dreamweaver 4 also provides two exciting new interactive image features, namely Flash text and Flash buttons. Both of these interactive image features can be created directly in Dreamweaver, adding the dynamic animation of Flash — without purchasing or learning how to operate the Flash program.

In this part . . .

Creating a Link from an Image

You can make an image interactive by simply making it a link. Clicking an image set up as a link causes the user to jump somewhere else in the site or on the Web. Create a link from an image as follows:

1. Select the image in the Document window. Doing so opens the Image Property inspector. If the inspector does not appear, open it by choosing Windows⇨Properties from the Menu bar.

2. In the Image Property inspector, click the Link folder to open the Select File dialog box.

3. Browse to select the page you want to link to. If the link is outside the current folder, click the arrow tab beside the Look In box and browse to select the file you want. Alternatively, you may enter a Web address in the URL box at the bottom of the Select File dialog box.

4. Click the Select button. The dialog box closes, and the link is activated.

You can't check an image link in Dreamweaver, but you can test that an image link is working by previewing your page in any browser. Just choose File⇨Preview in Browser from the Menu bar or click the Preview in Browser button.

Drawing Image Maps

Image maps are images with regions called *hotspots* — active areas of an image that a user can click to open a link to another Web page or activate a behavior. (*See also* Part VII.) Hotspots can be shaped like rectangles, circles, or polygons (irregular objects).

Adding an image map

You can add an image map to a Web page by using the same procedure for adding any image. *See also* "Adding an Image" in Part V for details.

Creating a hotspot

Use the following procedure for creating a hotspot:

1. Select the image that you want to add a hotspot to. The Image Properties inspector appears. If the inspector does not appear, open it by choosing Window⇨Properties from the Menu bar. If the bottom half of the Image Properties inspector is not

visible, click the Expander button (the down arrow in the bottom-right corner).

2. In the Map area of the Image Properties inspector, click a Hotspot button for the shape you want to draw. You can choose among a rectangle, a circle, and a polygon. Your mouse pointer becomes a crosshair cursor when you move it over the image.

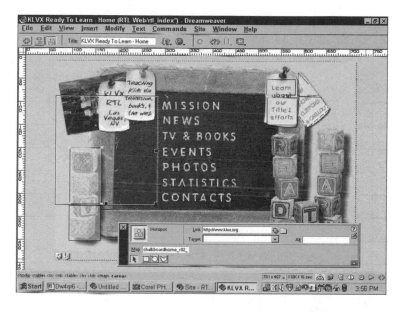

3. Draw the hotspot according to the shape you select:

   - **Circle or rectangle:** Click your crosshair cursor on the image and drag to create a hotspot. Release the mouse button when your hotspot reaches your desired dimensions. The area you draw is highlighted light blue, and the Hotspot Property inspector appears.

   - **Polygon:** Click your crosshair cursor on the image once for each point. Click the Arrow tool in the Image Properties inspector to close the shape. The area you draw is highlighted light blue, and the Hotspot Property inspector appears.

4. In the Hotspot Property inspector, supply the following information:

- **Map:** Enter a unique name for the hotspot in the Map.

- **Link:** Enter a URL or the name of an HTML file you want to open when the user clicks the hotspot. Alternatively, you can click the folder and browse to select the link from your files. Completing this box is optional — you may instead choose to attach a behavior to the hotspot. (*See also* Part VII.)

- **Target:** Complete this box if you entered a link in the Link box. Click the tab and select from the drop-down list a target window where your selected link will appear. You can select from the following choices: _blank, _parent, _self, and _top. If you have created frames, you can also select a frame name from this list. (*See also* Part X.)

- **Alt:** Enter the text you want to show when the user points the mouse to the hotspot.

Your hotspot is added to the image, and the associated HTML code is added to the page.

You must preview your page in a browser to check that a hotspot is functioning properly.

You can't draw a polygon hotspot on an image in a layer. You must first take the image out of the layer, then draw the hotspot, and reinsert the image into a layer.

Modifying a hotspot

Use the following procedure to edit a hotspot:

1. On an image in the Document window, table cell, or layer, click the hotspot you want to modify. The Hotspot Property inspector appears. If the inspector does not appear, open it by choosing Window⇨Properties from the Menu bar.

2. Edit any information you want to change in the Hotspot Property inspector.

3. Reshape any hotspot by clicking the Arrow tool in the Hotspot Properties inspector and dragging your mouse.

4. Delete a hotspot by clicking it and then pressing the Delete key on your keyboard.

The associated HTML page code for your hotspot is modified according to your changes.

Generating Flash Text

Dreamweaver 4 provides you a simple new way to build basic Flash text into your Web page without using the Flash program. *Flash text* appears as text that changes colors when the user rolls the mouse pointer over it.

Adding Flash text

To add Flash text, follow these steps:

1. Click in the Document window, table cell, or layer in which you want to add Flash text.

2. Select the Insert Flash Text button from the Common Objects panel to open the Insert Flash Text dialog box. If the panel doesn't show, open it by choosing Properties⇨ Objects from the Menu bar. Alternatively, you can choose Insert⇨Interactive Objects⇨Flash Text from the Menu bar.

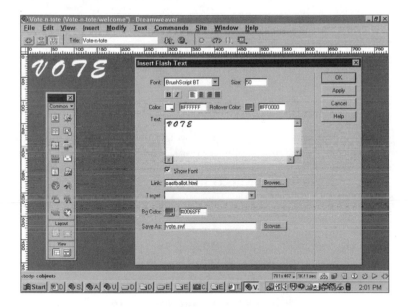

3. In the Insert Flash Text dialog box, select a text font from the Font drop-down list.

4. Enter a point size for your text in the Size box.

5. If you want, format the text. You can click the Bold button and/or Italics button. You can also click an alignment button. Alignment choices are left, center, right, and justify.

6. Select a Color and a Rollover Color by clicking the color swatch in each area and selecting a color from the color palette that appears.

7. Enter your actual text in the Text box. Click to check the Show Font check box if you want to view the Text box in your selected font.

8. In the Link box, enter a URL or the name of the page you want to appear when the user clicks the Flash text. Alternatively, you may click the Browse button to select a page from your files.

9. In the Target area, click the tab and select from the drop-down list a target window where the link will appear. If you have created frames, you can select a frame name from this list, or you can select from the following choices: _blank, _parent, _self, and _top (*See also* Part X.)

10. Select a Background color by clicking the Bg Color swatch and selecting a color from the color palette that appears.

    The *Bg Color* is the background color on which your Flash text is matted.

11. Enter a name for your Flash text in the Save As box or click the Browse button to select a name from your files.

    You must save Flash text with an `.swf` extension.

12. Click OK to create your Flash text and close the dialog box.

Dreamweaver creates and adds your Flash text to the Document window, and it updates your HTML page code to reflect the addition.

Changing Flash text

You can change a Flash text object you already created by simply double-clicking the object in the Document window. Doing so opens the Insert Flash Text dialog box where you can change your text as I describe in "Adding Flash text" earlier in this section. After you make changes to the Flash text object, you must resave the object.

Modifying Flash text features

You can add additional features to Flash text as follows:

1. In the Document window, select the Flash text object you want to enhance. The Flash Text Property inspector appears. If the inspector does not appear, open it by choosing Window⇨ Properties from the Menu bar.

2. In the Flash Text Property inspector, modify any available Flash text attributes.

   Most attributes are identical to those for a regular image. (***See also*** Part V for information on setting image attributes.) Attributes specific to Flash text consist of the following:

   • **ID:** Enter a name for the optional ActiveX ID parameter. See documentation on the Flash program for details.

   • **Quality:** Select a quality parameter for the Flash text object from the drop-down list. Quality sets the level of anti-aliasing during movie playback. You can select one of four options — Low, Auto Low, Auto High, or High. Low gives precedence to playback speed over quality, while high (the default) gives precedence to playback quality over speed. See documentation on the Flash program for details.

   • **Scale:** Select a scale parameter from the drop-down list. Scale defines browser placement of the movie when width and height values are percentages. You can choose Default (Show all), No Border, or Exact Fit. The default shows the entire movie in the specified area. Borders may be added on two sides of the movie to maintain the aspect ratio. No Border also maintains the aspect ratio but may crop two sides of the movie to do so. Exact Fit fills the specified area with the movie, without regard for the aspect ratio. See documentation on the Flash program for details.

   • **Parameters:** Click this button to open the Parameters dialog box where you can add, modify, and delete additional Flash attributes of your Flash text object. For example, you can set up the attributes that control how the object plays and interacts with other content in the Document window. See documentation on the Flash program for details.

Dreamweaver updates the Flash text object in the Document window, and the HTML page code changes to reflect your modifications.

You need to know something about working with the Flash program if you plan to add parameters that extend the animation features of the Flash text object.

Playing Flash text

To play Flash text, select the text in the Document window to open the Flash Text Property inspector. In the Property inspector, click the Play button to view your Flash text as it appears in the browser window. Click the Stop button when you finish.

Including Fireworks HTML

You can easily include HTML page code and images created in Macromedia's Fireworks program in your Web page as follows:

1. Click in the Document window, table cell, or layer in which you want to add the Fireworks HTML.

 2. Click the Insert Fireworks HTML button from the Common Objects panel to open the Insert Fireworks HTML dialog box. If the panel doesn't show, open it by choosing Properties⇨Objects from the Menu bar. Alternatively, you may choose Insert⇨Interactive Objects⇨Fireworks HTML from the Menu bar to open the panel.

3. In the Insert Fireworks HTML dialog box, enter the name of the file you want to insert into your page or click the Browse button to select the HTML document from your files.

4. In the Options area, select the check box if you want to delete the original Fireworks HTML page code after it's added to your document. Deleting the original Fireworks HTML page code helps keep your site root folder tidy by removing the now redundant file.

5. Click OK to apply your selections and then close the dialog box.

Dreamweaver updates your HTML page code to reflect the addition of the Fireworks HTML.

Inserting Rollovers

A *rollover* is an image that appears to change whenever the user rolls the mouse pointer over it. Rollovers add interactivity to a Web page by helping users know what parts of the page link to other Web pages.

A rollover is actually two images — one for normal display on a page (the original image) and one that is slightly modified for display when the image is rolled over (the rollover image). You can modify an image by changing the color or position, adding a glow or a shadow, or you can add another graphic — such as a dog changing from sleeping to wide-awake.

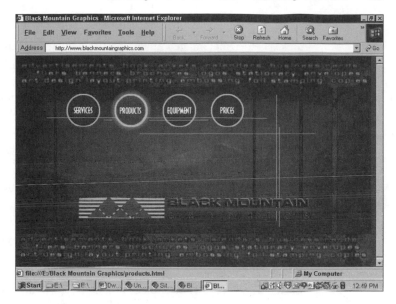

Insert a rollover by following these steps:

1. Click either inside the Document window, inside a table cell, or inside a layer in which you want to insert the rollover.

2. Click the Insert Rollover Image button from the Common Objects panel to open the Insert Rollover Image dialog box. If the panel doesn't show, open it by choosing Properties⇨Objects from the Menu bar. Alternatively, you may choose Insert⇨ Interactive Images⇨Rollover Image from the Menu bar.

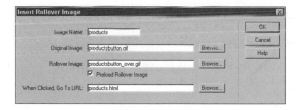

3. In the Insert Rollover Image dialog box, enter a name for the rollover in the Image Name box.

The rollover is referred to by this name in the HTML page code. Keep in mind that this rollover name refers to the combined original image/rollover image pair.

4. Enter the name of the original image file in the Original Image box or click the Browse button to select an image from your files. The original image appears on the page when the user's mouse pointer is not over the rollover.

5. Enter the name of the rollover image file in the Rollover Image box, or click the Browse button to select an image from your files. The rollover image appears on the page when the user's mouse pointer is over the rollover.

6. Check the Preload Rollover Image check box to set up the behavior that loads the rollover image when the Web page loads. This feature also makes the rollover action appear without delay to users as they move the mouse pointer over the original image.

7. In the When Clicked, Go To URL text box, enter a URL or the name for the page you want to appear when the user clicks the rollover. Alternatively, you may click the Browse button to select a page from your files.

8. Click OK to accept your choices and close the dialog box.

Dreamweaver inserts the original image into your Document window and adds the code for the rollover to your HTML page code.

To check the rollover, you must preview your page in a browser. Do so by choosing File➪Preview in Browser from the Menu bar or by clicking the Preview in Browser button and using your mouse to point to the original image.

As with all images, you can't create the original image or the rollover image directly in Dreamweaver — only in an image-editing program, such as Fireworks.

Making Flash Buttons

The latest version of Dreamweaver offers a nifty new way to add interactivity to your Web pages — by using Flash buttons. Flash buttons are actually miniature movies that play when the user mouses over them. Like Flash text, you don't need to know anything about the Flash program to create these animated little buttons at the basic level. Dreamweaver 4 does that work for you. But if you want to get fancy and incorporate additional motion or playback features, you may want to put your hands on the nearest Flash manual.

Adding a Flash button

To add a Flash button, follow these steps:

1. Click in the Document window, table cell, or layer in which you want to add a Flash Button.

2. Click the Insert Flash Button button from the Common Objects panel to open the Insert Flash Button dialog box. If the panel doesn't show, open it by choosing Properties⇨Objects from the Menu bar. Alternatively, you may choose Insert⇨ Interactive Objects⇨Flash Button from the Menu bar.

3. At the Insert Flash Button dialog box, scroll through the button selections in the Style list and click to select a style. You can preview the style in the Sample area of the dialog box — just point to the sample with your mouse to see the Flash button play.

4. If your selected button has a placeholder for text, enter the text you want to appear on the button in the Button Text area.

5. Select a font for your Flash button text from the Font drop-down list.

6. Enter a point size for your text in the Size box.

7. In the Link box, enter a URL or the name for the page you want to appear when the user clicks the Flash button. Alternatively, you may click the Browse button to select a page from your files.

8. In the Target area, click the tab and select from the drop-down list a target window where the URL will appear. You can select from the following choices: _blank, _parent, _self, and _top. If you have created frames, you can also select a frame name from this list. (*See also* Part X.)

9. Select a Background color by clicking the Bg Color swatch and selecting a color from the color palette that appears. Alternatively, you may enter a hexadecimal color code in the Bg Color box. The *Bg Color* is the color on which your Flash button is matted.

10. Enter a name for your Flash button in the Save As box or click the Browse button to select a name from your files. You must save the Flash button with an .swf extension.

11. Click OK to create your Flash button and then close the dialog box.

Dreamweaver inserts the Flash button into your Document window and adds the reference code to your HTML page code.

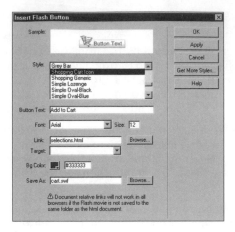

 Get new Flash buttons on the Macromedia Dreamweaver Web site by clicking the Get More Styles button in the Insert Flash Button dialog box.

Changing a Flash button

To change a Flash button object you have already created, simply double-click the object in the Document window. Doing so opens the Insert Flash Button dialog box where you can change your button as I describe in "Adding a Flash button" earlier in this section. After you make changes to the Flash button object, you must resave the object.

Modifying Flash button features

You can add additional features to a Flash button as follows:

1. In the Document window, click to select the Flash button object you want to enhance. The Flash Text Property inspector appears. If the inspector does not appear, open it by choosing Window➪Properties from the Menu bar.

2. At the Flash button Property inspector, modify any of the available Flash button attributes.

Most attributes are identical to those for a regular image. (*See also* Part V for information on setting image attributes.) Attributes specific to a Flash button are the same as those listed for Flash text in "Modifying Flash text features" earlier in this part.

Dreamweaver updates the Flash button object in the Document window and updates the code for the button in your HTML page code.

Playing a Flash button

To play a Flash button, select the button in the Document window to open the Flash Button Property inspector. In the Property inspector, click the Play button to view your Flash button as it appears in the browser window. Click the Stop button after you finish.

Setting Up a Navigation Bar

A *Navigation bar* is a group of buttons that users can access to move throughout your Web site. Buttons within a Navigation bar may present users with options such as moving backwards, moving forwards, returning to the home page, or jumping to specific pages within the site.

Each button in a Navigation bar possesses properties similar to a rollover in that the button *changes state* — or appears differently — based on where the user is positioning the mouse pointer. However, a Navigation bar button may possess as many as four different states:

- ✓ **Up:** The original state of the button.

- ✓ **Over:** How the button appears when the mouse points to it.

- ✓ **Down:** How the button appears when the mouse pointer clicks it.

- ✓ **Over While Down:** How the button appears when the mouse points to it after being clicked.

A Navigation bar differs from individual rollovers in that clicking a Navigation Bar button in the Down state causes all other buttons in the bar to revert to the Up state.

Creating a new Navigation bar

Create a Navigation bar as follows:

1. Select the Insert Navigation Bar button from the Common Objects panel. If the panel doesn't show, open it by choosing Properties⇨Objects from the Menu bar. Alternatively, you may choose Insert⇨Interactive Objects⇨Navigation Bar from the Menu bar.

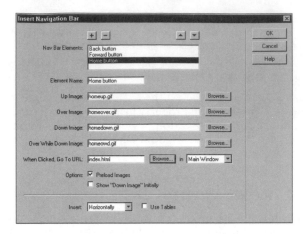

2. At the Insert Navigation Bar dialog box, enter a name for the first button in the Element Name box. The new button appears in the Nav Bar Elements box.

3. For each state of the button — Up Image, Over Image, Down Image, and Over While Down Image — enter the name of the image file you want to use in the associated field. Alternatively, you may click the Browse button for each field and select an image from your files. You must supply the Up Image — all other states are optional and may be left blank.

4. In the When Clicked, Go To URL box, enter a URL or the name for the page you want to appear when the user clicks the Navigation bar button. Alternatively, you may click the Browse button to select a page from your files.

5. Click the drop-down list tab and then select a target window where you want the URL to appear. If you are not using frames, the only option is to use the Main window.

6. Click the (+) button to add another Navigation bar button.

   Repeat Steps 2–5 to format the new button. *Note:* You can remove any button already created by clicking its name in the Nav Bar Elements box and clicking the Remove (-) button. Reorder the sequence of the buttons by clicking a button name in the Nav Bar Elements box and clicking the up or down arrow.

7. In the Options area, select the Preload Images check box if you want to set up the behavior that loads all states of the button image when the page loads. Doing so causes the change of state actions to appear without delay when the user interacts with the button.

8. To set the current button to appear in the Down state when the user first sees the Navigation bar, select the Show "Down Image" Initially check box in the Options area.

9. In the Insert list box, click the tab and select from the drop-down list to position the Navigation bar either Horizontally or Vertically.

10. To set up the button images in a table format, select the Use Tables check box.

11. Click OK to accept your choices and then close the dialog box.

Dreamweaver inserts the Navigation bar into your Document window and then adds the code for the bar to your HTML page code.

To check the Navigation bar, you must preview your page in a browser. Choose File⇨Preview in Browser from the Menu bar or click the Preview in Browser button and then use your mouse to point to the buttons.

You cannot create the Navigation bar buttons in Dreamweaver — you need an image-editing program to accomplish this task, such as Macromedia's Fireworks program. This program works especially well and even offers a library of premade navigation buttons with all four states.

You do not need to use all four Navigation bar button states — eliminating Over While Down or creating only Up and Down works just fine.

Modifying a Navigation bar

To change elements of a Navigation bar you already created, choose Modify⇨Navigation Bar from the Menu bar. Doing so opens the Modify Navigation Bar dialog box where you can make edits.

The Modify Navigation Bar dialog box is nearly identical to the Insert Navigation Bar dialog box, except that you can no longer change the orientation of the bar or access the Use Tables check box.

Part VII

Building Navigation and Activity

Navigation offers users the ability to peruse your site — and millions of other sites — in any sequence that they choose. Using links on your page enables users to jump forward and backward on your page or to any other Web page that you create a link to. You can even build e-mail links that let users write and send e-mail messages to whatever addresses you set up.

Also, you can build activity into your Web pages by incorporating behaviors in your page design. With behaviors, you can precisely control how and when page information is presented. For example, you can attach a show/hide layer behavior to a layer so that a user mouse click changes the layer's visibility — under certain circumstances the content of the layer shows, but under other conditions the content is hidden.

In this part . . .

Adding Behaviors

A *behavior* is an action that is executed in a Web browser whenever the user performs some sort of event. Most, but not all, behaviors serve some sort of navigational function. For example, one of the most popular behaviors is the Swap Image behavior that you use to create a rollover image. Whenever the user performs a mouse-over event, the Swap Image action is executed. The behavior doesn't enable the user to navigate to a new destination, but the behavior-accompanying link serves to direct the navigation. In this example, the behavior signals to the user that the link is present.

Behaviors are browser-specific. Not all behaviors function similarly — or function at all — in all browsers. Newer browsers can display a greater number of behaviors than can older browsers. When you set up a behavior, Dreamweaver provides you with a list of target browsers to help you determine what users in your target audience will see when they view your page.

For an extensive list and comprehensive description of behaviors, refer to *HTML For Dummies Quick Reference*, 2nd Edition by Deborah S. Ray and Eric J. Ray (IDG Books Worldwide, Inc.) and *JavaScript For Dummies Quick Reference*, by Emily Vander Veer (IDG Books Worldwide, Inc.).

Attaching a behavior

Follow these steps to attach a behavior:

1. In the Document window, select the object that you want to attach a behavior to. To attach a behavior to the entire page, select the <body> tag from the Tag Selector in the bottom-left corner of the Document window.

2. Open the Behaviors panel by choosing Window⇨Behaviors from the Menu bar. Alternatively, you can click the Show Behaviors icon on either Launcher. (*See also* "The Big Picture.")

3. Click the add (+) button in the Behaviors panel. Doing so opens a pop-up menu of available behaviors. Choices include Check Plugin, Play Sound, Popup Message, Preload Images, and many others.

4. Choose a behavior from the pop-up menu.

5. Complete the information in the dialog box that appears for your selected behavior.

6. Click OK.

Dreamweaver adds the behavior to your page and lists it in the Behaviors panel. Additionally, the associated HTML and JavaScript codes are added to your page code.

You can obtain additional behaviors from the Web — beyond the basic ones with which Dreamweaver ships — by choosing the Get More Behaviors option in the Behaviors pop-up menu.

Choosing an event

An *event* is what the user does in order to execute a behavior on a Web page. Adding a behavior causes an event to be automatically assigned, but you have the option of changing this assignment in the Behaviors panel.

To assign an event for a behavior, follow these steps:

1. In the Behaviors panel, select the currently assigned event for the behavior you want to work on. If the Behaviors panel doesn't show, open it by choosing Window➪Behaviors from the Menu bar.

2. In the Events pane, click the down-arrow button next to the currently assigned event.

3. From the events pop-up menu that appears, choose Show Events For and select a level of browser compatibility you want to target. A greater number of users can view your page if you use an older browser version. However, if you do use an older version, fewer behaviors are available.

4. From the events pop-up menu, choose an event.

   Menu options vary depending on the behavior and target browser but may consist of choices, such as OnMouseOver and OnClick. Most event names are descriptive; however, you may encounter the following less obvious event choices:

   • **OnAbort:** Occurs when the user clicks the browser's Stop button, which interrupts page or image loading.

   • **OnBlur:** Occurs when the user moves away from an object that was previously the focus of interaction.

   • **OnError:** Occurs when a browser error takes place.

   • **OnFocus:** Occurs when the user interacts with an object, which makes it the focus of activity.

   • **OnLoad:** Occurs when a Web page or a page image completes loading.

   • **OnUnload:** Occurs when a user leaves the current Web page.

   Dreamweaver modifies the event in the Behaviors panel and the associated HTML and JavaScript code for your page.

Choosing an action

Adding a behavior automatically assigns one or more actions in the Behaviors panel. You cannot change an action without changing the associated behavior. Dreamweaver 4 offers you 25 standard actions, and each action possesses its own dialog box where you can specify attributes regarding how the action is executed.

Action	What the Action Enables You to Do
Call JavaScript	Execute any JavaScript function
Change Property	Alter attributes of certain tags, including certain layer and form tags
Check Browser	Check user's browser version and redirect certain users to alternative URLs
Check Plugin	Check availability of plugins in user's browser and redirect certain users to alternative URLs
Control Shockwave or Flash	Command Shockwave or Flash movies via external controls
Drag Layer	Allow users to drag and drop layers on a Web page
Go to URL	Open a URL in the frame you Indicate; useful for updating two or more frames simultaneously
Jump Menu	Edit an existing Jump Menu object
Jump Menu Go	Add an image as a Go button
Open Browser Window	Open a link in a browser window with attributes you customize, including size and user ability to resize
Play Sound	Add background music to a page
Popup Message	Send an alert or message to users In a small window
Preload Images	Cache images such as rollovers to speed their display on a page
Set Nav Bar Image	Edit an existing Navigation bar object
Set Text	Interactively update text contents of a frame, layer, status bar, or text field
Show/Hide Layers	Change the visibility of a layer
Swap Image	Create rollover swap of images
Swap Image/Restore	Create rollover swap of images and then return the image to the original state
Timeline	Control Timeline activities via Play Timeline, Stop Timeline, and Go to Timeline Frame
Validate Form	Check that a user has completed a form correctly

Deleting a behavior

To delete a behavior, follow these steps:

1. In the Document window, select the object that has attached to it the behavior you want to delete. To delete a behavior that is attached to the entire page, select the <body> tag from the Tag Selector in the bottom-left corner of the Document window.

2. Open the Behaviors panel inspector by choosing Window➪Behaviors from the Menu bar or by clicking the Behavior icon from any Launcher.

 3. Click the Remove (–) sign in the Behaviors panel.

Dreamweaver removes the behavior from the Document window and also updates the associated HTML and JavaScript code for your page.

Sequencing multiple behaviors

You can attach multiple behaviors to your Web page or to an object on your page by repeating the steps in "Attaching a behavior" as many times as you want. By default, multiple behaviors for an element on your Web page are listed alphabetically according to event names. Behaviors execute in the order in which they are listed. However, you can resequence behaviors that have the same event by clicking any of these behaviors in the Behaviors panel and clicking the up- or down-arrow button in the panel. For example, you can resequence the order of two or more behaviors that have mouse over events.

Creating Links

You can set up virtually any object on a Web page as a *link* so that when users click the object, they navigate to another location. Links are most frequently created from text and images.

Create a link by following these steps:

1. In the Document window, select the image or text you want to set up as a link. Doing so opens the Image Property inspector or Text Property inspector. If the inspector does not appear, open it by choosing Windows➪Properties from the Menu bar.

2. In the Property inspector, click the Link folder to open the Select File dialog box.

3. Browse to select the page you want to link to. If the link is out-side the current folder, click the arrow tab beside the Look In box and browse to select the file you want. Alternatively, you may enter a Web address in the URL box at the bottom of the Select File dialog box.

4. Click the Select button.

Dreamweaver closes the dialog box and activates the link. The associated HTML code is added to your page.

To check that a link works properly, preview your page in any browser by choosing File⇨Preview in Browser from the Menu bar or by clicking the Preview in Browser button.

Text links are distinguished with formatting you set in your Page Properties (*see also* Part I) — unless you override the formatting with CSS Styles (*see also* Part IV). However, image links may not be immediately obvious to a user. While examining your page in a browser, the mouse cursor changes from a pointer to a selection hand whenever it encounters a link.

Establishing E-Mail Links

An *e-mail link* is a link that opens a new e-mail message window when a user clicks it. The New Message window contains the user's e-mail address in the From box and whatever e-mail address you specify in the To box. For users who haven't configured their browsers to handle e-mail, the From box is blank.

The text of the e-mail link on the page can be different from the actual address to which the link connects.

Set up an e-mail link as follows:

1. In the Document window, select the text that you want to make an e-mail link. Alternatively, you can just position your cursor in the Document window or any text object where you want to insert the link.

2. Choose Insert⇨E-Mail Link from the Menu bar or click the Insert E-Mail Link button on the Common Objects panel. If the Objects panel doesn't show, open it by choosing Window⇨Objects from the Menu bar.

3. In the Insert E-Mail Link dialog box that appears, enter the text you want to display for the link in the Text box. If you selected text in Step 1, that text appears in the Text box.

4. In the Insert E-Mail Link dialog box, type in the E-Mail box the e-mail address where you want messages sent.

5. Click OK.

Dreamweaver adds the e-mail link to your Web page and updates the HTML code to reflect your addition.

Additionally, selecting the e-mail link in the Document window causes the Text Property inspector to show the mailto: address you establish in the Link box.

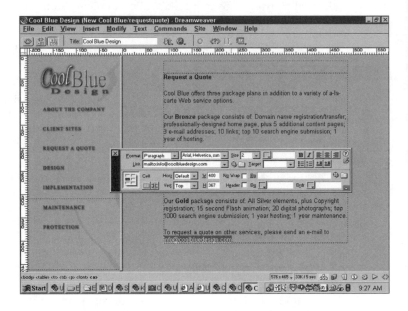

To check that the e-mail link is operational, you must preview the page in a Web browser.

Users who have not configured their Web browsers to handle e-mail may not be able to successfully use your e-mail links. For this reason, you can make the Text and E-mail address the same in the Insert E-Mail Link dialog box. Giving users the actual e-mail address enables them to use whatever e-mail program they want to contact you.

Using Named Anchors

When you want to create a navigational link that connects users not just to a page, but to a specific location on the page, you can create a *named anchor*. Named anchors are frequently used for jumping to exact positions within a large block of text so that users don't have to scroll through sentence after sentence to find the information they need. Setting up named anchors is especially useful when creating links from a directory or a table of contents to the content it presents.

Inserting an anchor tag

Place an anchor anywhere on your Web page as follows:

1. In the Document window, click your mouse cursor at the position you want to insert the named anchor.

2. Click the Insert Named Anchor button on the Invisibles Objects panel or choose Insert⇨Invisible Tags⇨Named Anchor from the Menu bar. If the Objects panel doesn't show, open it by choosing Window⇨Objects from the Menu bar.

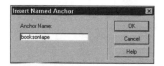

3. In the resulting Insert Named Anchor dialog box, type a name in the Anchor Name box.

4. Click OK.

Dreamweaver adds the named anchor to your Web page and updates the HTML code to reflect your addition.

 If you can't see the named anchor tag, you may have the Invisible Elements feature turned off. *See also* "The Big Picture" for information on turning on the ability to view Invisible Elements in your Dreamweaver document.

 It's a good idea to insert the named anchor tag slightly above the actual position where you want the link to target. Doing so gives your targeted content a little padding on top. Otherwise, the top of your image or your first line of text appears flush with the top of the browser window.

Linking to a Named Anchor

To link to a named anchor, follow the procedure outlined in the "Creating Links" section with the following modifications:

✔ **Linking to a named anchor on the current page:** In the Link box of the Property inspector, type a pound sign followed by the anchor name.

✔ **Linking to a named anchor on a different page:** In the Link box of the Property inspector, type the HTML page name followed by a pound sign and then the anchor name.

As of this writing, the latest version of Netscape Navigator (Version 6.0) supports linking to named anchors on the current page — not other pages.

Removing an anchor tag

To delete an anchor tag, you can click the tag in the Document window and then press the Delete key.

Renaming an anchor tag

To change the name of an existing anchor tag, click the tag in the Document window to open the Named Anchor Property inspector. If the inspector does not appear, open it by choosing Window⇨ Properties from the Menu bar. Type a new name for the anchor in the Name box.

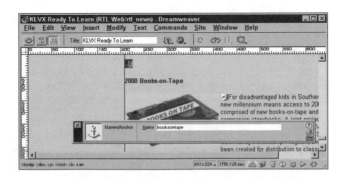

Part VIII

Animating Your Pages

Have you ever created a children's flip-book? If so, Dreamweaver 4 comes with a feature just for you — timeline animation. Generating timeline animation means that you aren't limited to designing with static images. You can play the role of animation director and add eye-catching motion and activity to any page in your site.

Creating animation in Dreamweaver hinges on manipulating the timeline. You use the timeline to define which objects show up on your page, how they are positioned, and what other media are playing anytime a user is viewing your Web page. The timeline enables you to change all these parameters from one second to the next, creating a motion enriched page — without the drudgery of generating true animation.

In this part . . .

About Timelines

You can use the Timelines panel to record and playback Dreamweaver animation.

Attributes of the Timelines panel

Open the Timelines panel by choosing Window➪Timelines from the Menu bar.

Behavior channel   Playback head

Timeline files   Playback controls

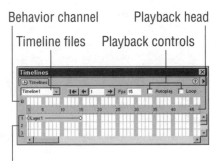

Animation channels

The following features appear on the Timelines panel:

- ✔ **Timeline controls:** Enables you to select which timeline you want to view and to control the playback of the timeline. This area consists of the Timeline files drop-down list, the Rewind button, the Back button, the Current Frame Number text box, the Play button, the Frame Rate (fps) text box, the Autoplay check box, and the Loop check box.

- ✔ **Behavior channel:** Enables you to attach behaviors to specific frames of animations in the timeline you select. (*See also* "Triggering Timeline Behaviors" in this part, and all of Part VII).

- ✔ **Frames:** Displays the frame numbers for your selected timeline. You can click any frame number to display that frame. The current frame is indicated by the pink playback head. Clicking and dragging the playback head plays the frames as you drag.

- ✔ **Animation channels:** Enables you to add layers and animate layers on a channel. You can create multiple channels that run simultaneously or start and stop at frames you choose. You cannot animate the same layer on different channels simultaneously.

Functions of the timeline

Dreamweaver can't render animation like what you see in the movies, but it can help you create motion on your Web pages without a lot of headache. Here's what the timeline can accomplish:

- ✓ *Simple animation* that displays in a Web browser at approximately 15 frames per second (fps). For comparison, animation films show 24 fps. Note that the display rate is approximate and is actually based on the abilities of the user's system.

- ✓ *Layer manipulation,* including the ability to change a layer's position, size, visibility, and z-index (stacking position). (*See also* Part II.)

- ✓ *Behavior triggering,* meaning that you can set up a series of behaviors to execute at various points along the timeline.

- ✓ *Image revelation,* in which you may choose to change the source of an image to show and hide several images over a period of time, effectively creating a Web slide show. Images do not have to be located in layers to be animated in this fashion.

Guidelines for applying the timeline

Before you generate timeline animations, you must consider these general rules:

- ✓ Only Web users with 4.0 or later browsers can view timeline animations.

- ✓ To create motion animation for an object on a timeline, it must be contained within a layer. Without the absolute positioning of layers, motion animation is not possible. (*See also* Part II.)

- ✓ You can use the Timelines panel to change the source attributes of images not enclosed in layers. Doing so enables you to cause images to appear and disappear on your Web page over a period of time.

- ✓ You can run multiple animations on a single timeline.

- ✓ You can run multiple timelines to animate different layers simultaneously.

- ✓ Multiple, simultaneous animations cannot be applied to a single layer in any way. (In other words, no walking and chewing gum at the same time.)

Adding and Deleting Objects on a Timeline

The first step in creating a timeline animation is to add the layer or image that you want to animate to a timeline. Added objects can be deleted at any time.

Adding an object to a timeline

To add an object to a timeline, follow these steps:

1. Choose Window⇨Timelines from the Menu bar to access the Timelines panel.

2. In the Timelines panel, select the timeline you want to work on from the Timeline Name drop-down list.

3. In the Document window, select the layer or image you want to animate.

4. Add your selection to the timeline by using one of the following methods:

   - Choose Modify⇨Timeline⇨Add Object to Timeline from the Menu bar. Doing so adds an Animation bar to one of the channels. The Animation bar starts at the frame position of the playback head. The first Animation bar you create is placed on Animation Channel 1, the second animation bar is placed on Channel 2, and so on.

   - Drag the layer or image to an Animation channel on the timeline. You can drag the layer to any Animation channel and any start frame.

   Regardless of the method you choose, a 15-frame Animation bar is created, with keyframes included on the first and last frames. The name of the layer or image labels the newly created Animation bar.

5. Repeat Steps 2 through 4 to add other layers and images to the timeline.

Animation bar

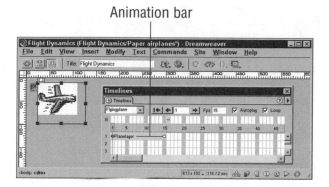

 The drag-and-drop method of adding layers and images to the time-line is easier to use and more flexible than the Menu bar method.

 Name your layers and images something more descriptive than the default names (Layer 1, or Image 1) so that you can better distinguish Animation bars in a timeline.

Deleting an object from a timeline

To delete an object from a timeline, simply select its Animation bar and choose Modify⇨Timeline⇨Remove Object from the Menu bar or just press the Delete key.

Adjusting Animation Bars

Each Animation bar defines the animation of a single object over a period of time. You can adjust defining attributes of your Animation bars.

Adding a frame to an Animation bar

You may choose to insert frames into an existing Animation bar to lengthen the duration of playback for the bar or to cause the animated object to hold its position for a short period of time before continuing to move. To add a frame to an Animation bar, click the Animation bar at the position you want to add a frame and choose Modify⇨Timeline⇨Add Frame from the Menu bar. Alternatively, right-click (Windows) or Control+click (Macintosh) and choose Add Frame from the pop-up menu.

Note that adding frames between two keyframes in an Animation bar possessing several keyframes changes the proportional spacing of the keyframes.

Changing the play time of an Animation bar

Click and drag the starting or ending keyframe of the Animation bar to adjust the number of frames (the length of the bar) as needed. The maximum length of an Animation bar is 300 frames. Keyframes in the bar maintain their proportional positions as you drag.

The number of frames and the frame rate (fps) define how many seconds your Animation bar plays — in theory. The actual playtime depends on the limitations of the user's system. For example, a 15-fps frame rate causes a 30-frame animation bar to play for 2 seconds.

Don't set your frame rate higher than 15 fps because users' systems are unlikely to accommodate higher playback rates.

Deleting a frame from an Animation bar

Click the Animation bar at the position you want to delete a frame and choose Modify➪Timeline➪Remove Frame from the Menu bar. Alternatively, right-click (Windows) or Control-click (Macintosh) and choose Remove Frame from the pop-up menu.

Repositioning an animation bar

Click and drag the bar to an open area on any Animation channel. A timeline can have as many as 32 animation channels.

Deleting an animation bar

Select the animation bar and choose Modify➪Timeline➪Remove Object from the Menu bar or just press the Delete key.

Altering Keyframes

A keyframe is as fundamental to constructing animation as a keystone is to constructing a building. A keyframe establishes a starting point from which subsequent construction progresses. A timeline can possess multiple keyframes spread throughout its sequence of frames. Each *keyframe* contains details about a particular stage of an object in an animation. Every time you set an object in motion along a new path or otherwise change its attributes on the timeline, you add a keyframe to define the change. The frames following a keyframe cause the object to continue along the same line of motion until a new keyframe is reached.

Keyframes are located on the first and last frames of every Animation bar and on as many frames in between as you need to accomplish your desired animation. For example, moving a layer along a straight-line path requires only two keyframes: one that defines where the layer starts and another that defines where it ends.

Adding a keyframe to an Animation bar

Click the Animation bar at the frame position where you want to add a keyframe. Then choose Modify⊅Timeline⊅Add Keyframe from the Menu bar. Alternatively, right-click (Windows) or Control-click (Macintosh) and then choose Add Keyframe from the pop-up menu.

Alternatively, you can select the Animation bar, hold down the Ctrl key, and then click at the frame position where you want to add a keyframe.

Changing a layer's position in a keyframe

Click the keyframe where you want to reposition a layer. The affected layer is displayed in the Document window in the position currently assigned by the keyframe. Change this position by dragging the layer to a new location. You can also use the arrow keys to make slight adjustments, or you can use the Layer Property inspector to set exact Left and Top position values. The new layer's position is registered by the keyframe.

Deleting a keyframe from an Animation bar

Click on the keyframe and choose Modify⊅Timeline⊅Remove Keyframe from the Menu bar. Alternatively, right-click (Windows) or Control-click (Macintosh) and choose Remove Keyframe from the pop-up menu. You cannot delete a starting or ending keyframe.

Repositioning a keyframe in an Animation bar

Click the keyframe and drag it to a new frame position. You can drag it only between — not across — other keyframes.

Building a Web Slide Show

A Web slide show displays and removes images in the same position on your page over a period of time. You can set the slide show to play automatically when the user opens the page (select Autoplay in the Timelines panel), or you can add a behavior to the Behavior channel that causes the slide show to play. To build a Web slide show, follow these steps:

1. Using an image-editing program of your choice, create the images you want to animate. All the images in a group will be placed on an animation bar together and must be the same size.

2. Choose Window⇨Timelines from the Menu bar to access the Timelines panel.

3. In the Timelines panel, select the timeline you want to work on from the Timeline Name drop-down list.

4. In the Document window, insert the first image from the same-size group of images. You can insert the image directly into the window, in a table cell, or in a layer. Images from the group are displayed in this location during the animation.

5. Click and drag the image to an Animation channel in the Timelines panel. A 15-frame Animation bar is created, with keyframes included on the first and last frames.

6. Set the frame rate, Autoplay, and Loop options as desired. Autoplay causes the slide show to play when the user opens the page, and Loop causes the slide show to play again when the end of the timeline animation is reached.

7. Add a keyframe at the frame on the Animation bar where you want the slide show image to change by selecting the frame and choosing Modify⇨Timeline⇨Add Keyframe from the Menu bar. The added keyframe is now the selected keyframe.

8. In the Image Properties inspector, browse in the Src folder to select a new image from your group of same-size images.

    Note: If the Image Properties inspector does not show, open it by choosing Window⇨Properties from the Menu bar.

9. Repeat Steps 7 and 8 to add more images to your slide show.

Dreamweaver updates your page code to include your slide show animation.

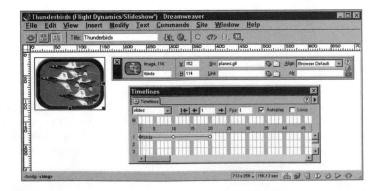

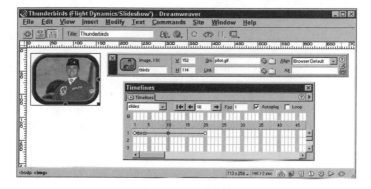

You can create as many slide show areas on your Web page as you want. Just create a new Animation bar for each slide show area and be sure that all the images you place on the bar are the same size. Different Animation bars can have images of different sizes.

Looping a Path

For a looped animation, the default number of loops is infinite — the animation keeps looping until the user closes the page. By default, the loop includes the entire range of frames, frame 1 to the final frame. However, you can set an exact number of loops and a specific start frame for the loop by using the following procedure:

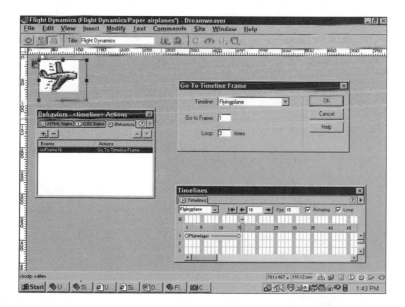

1. In the Timelines panel, select the Loop check box. If the Timelines panel does not show, then open it by choosing Window⇨Timelines from the Menu bar. The first time you select Loop, Dreamweaver displays an alert informing you that the Go To Timeline Frame is being added. The alert also advises you of the exact frame in the Behavior channel you must double-click to edit the action. You can disable the display of this alert by selecting the check box for Don't Show Me This Message Again. Click the OK button to proceed with adding the loop.

   A marker is placed in the Behavior channel indicating the addition of the loop. (The Behavior channel is the channel labeled *B* just above the frames in the Timelines panel.)

2. In the Behavior channel, double-click the frame containing the marker for the looping behavior.

   The Behaviors panel opens with the looping behavior selected. The Events pane displays an onFrame event, and the Actions pane displays a Go To Timeline Frame action.

3. Double-click the onFrame event. Doing so opens the Go To Timeline Frame dialog box.

4. In the Go to Timeline Frame dialog box, enter a frame number for where you want the loop to begin. The default frame is 1.

5. In the Loop box, enter a number for the number of loops you want your timeline animation to execute. The default is an empty box that causes the loop to execute an infinite number of times.

6. Click OK.

Dreamweaver updates your page code to reflect the loop modification you make.

Manipulating Timelines

You can add, delete, or rename timelines as needed.

Adding a timeline

Choose Modify⇨Timeline⇨Add Timeline from the Menu bar.

Deleting a timeline

Choose Modify⇨Timeline⇨Remove Timeline from the Menu bar.

Renaming a timeline

Open the timeline that you want to rename and choose
Modify⇨Timeline⇨Rename Timeline from the Menu bar. Enter a
new name in the Rename Timeline dialog box that appears and
then click OK. Alternatively, you can just enter a new name directly
in the Timeline Name box. The name must be a single word that
begins with a letter and consists of only alphanumeric characters.

Playing a Recorded Path

The Timelines panel provides playback controls that enable you to
control how you view a recorded animation path. Unlike many
other interactive functions in Dreamweaver, you don't have to preview pages in a browser to see how an animation looks. You can
use the timeline controls to preview your work directly in the
Document Window. The following table explains the function of
each control:

Timeline Control	Function
Rewind button	Moves the playback head backward to the first frame of the selected timeline.
Back button	Backs up the playback head by one frame; click and hold to play the timeline in reverse.
Frame indicator	Shows the position of the playback head; enter a frame number to jump to that frame.
Play button	Advances the playback head by one frame; click and hold to play the timeline start to finish
Fps text box	Sets the frame rate in frames per second at which the animation plays. To change the default rate of 15 fps, enter a number and press Enter (Windows) or Return (Macintosh).
Autoplay check box	When checked, causes the selected timeline to begin playing as soon as the page completely downloads in the browser.
Loop check box	When checked, causes the animation to repeat upon reaching the last frame. *See also* "Looping a Path."

Leave the Autoplay check box unchecked if you want the triggering event for playing the animation to be something other than downloading the page. But don't forget to attach a behavior that performs the triggering!

Recording a Freeform Path

Create an animation that moves a layer in a freeform path as follows:

1. Choose Window⇨Timelines from the Menu bar to access the Timelines panel.

2. In the Timelines panel, select the timeline you want to work on from the Timeline Name drop-down list.

3. In the Document window, select the layer you want to animate. The current location of the layer is the starting point for the animation. If you want a different starting point, reposition the layer now.

4. Choose Modify⇨Timeline⇨Record Path of Layer from the Menu bar. Alternatively, right-click (Windows) or Control-click (Macintosh) the layer and choose Record Path from the pop-up menu.

5. Click and drag the layer into the Document window to create any path you want. Doing so traces the path as you drag. The path follows the position of the top-left corner of the layer.

6. Release the mouse button to end recording the path. A new Animation bar for the recorded path appears in the Timelines panel. The length of the bar corresponds to the time you spent dragging the layer. Intervals during which you dragged slowly consist of more keyframes than those intervals during which you dragged rapidly.

Dreamweaver updates your page code to include the new path.

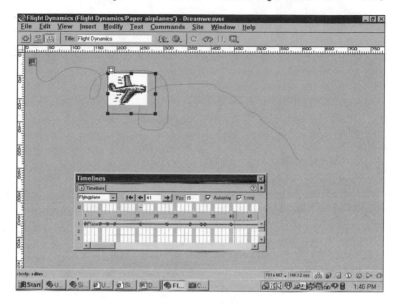

Recording a Linear Path

Create an animation that moves a layer in a straight line as follows:

1. Choose Window⇨Timelines from the Menu bar to access the Timelines panel.

2. In the Timelines panel, select the timeline you want to work on from the Timeline Name drop-down list.

3. In the Document window, select the layer you want to animate. The current location of the layer is the starting point for the animation. If you want a different starting point, reposition the layer now.

4. Drag the layer to the Timelines panel. You can drag the layer to any Animation channel and any start frame. By default, a 15-frame Animation bar is created, with keyframes included on the first and last frames.

5. Click the ending keyframe in the Animation bar and drag it to create the duration of animation you want.

6. In the Document window, drag the selected layer to its ending position. Dreamweaver draws a thin line that displays the animation path. For you caffeine junkies, you'll be happy to know that Dreamweaver automatically accounts for shaky hands and makes your line straight.

Dreamweaver adds the animation and updates the source code for your page.

To view your path, rewind to the start frame and click the Play button.

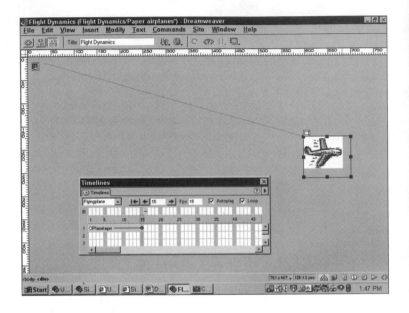

Triggering Timeline Behaviors

Including behaviors in your timeline animations enables you to create richer, more interactive Web pages.

In the simplest application of behaviors, you can set up an animation to start playing as soon as the page fully loads (the Autoplay feature) or to play repeatedly until the user closes the page (the Loop feature). These features use three behaviors to run, namely Play Timeline, Stop Timeline, and Go to Timeline Frame. But because the Autoplay and Loop features are used so frequently, you don't even have to work with the Behavior channel to set them up — they're preprogrammed so that you need only select their check boxes in the Timelines panel whenever you want to apply them.

You can also use behaviors to build much more advanced control over the events that cause your animation to execute. To do so, you must attach each behavior to your target timeline, then set the specific parameters of the behavior. For example, you can set an animation to play when a user clicks a hotspot on an image map or clicks to select a check box.

Attaching a behavior to a timeline

Use any of the following methods to attach a behavior to a timeline:

☑ Select the frame where you want to add a behavior and then choose Modify➪Timeline➪Add Behavior to Timeline from the Menu bar. Alternatively, you can right-click (Windows) or Control-click (Macintosh) and choose Add Behavior from the pop-up menu.

☑ In the Behavior channel, double-click the frame where you want to add a behavior. The Behavior channel is the channel labeled *B* just above the frames in the Timelines panel.

The Behaviors panel displays your added behavior in the Events pane. The added behavior indicates what frame it is attached to, such as onFrame30. The event can trigger multiple actions to take place.

Removing a behavior from a timeline

Remove a behavior from a timeline by selecting the behavior in the Behavior channel and choosing Modify➪Timeline➪Remove Behavior from the Menu bar. Alternatively, you can right-click (Windows) or Control-click (Macintosh) and choose Remove Behavior from the pop-up menu.

Setting up timeline behaviors

After attaching a behavior to a frame in your timeline, you can set up your animation to invoke any behavior. (*See also* Part VI for details on the function of available behaviors.) Three timeline-specific behaviors are available and consist of Go to Timeline Frame, Play Timeline, or Stop Timeline. You can add any of these timeline behaviors by following these steps:

1. In the Document window, select the object you want to serve as the trigger for the timeline behavior.

2. Choose Window➪Behaviors from the Menu bar. Alternatively, you can click the Behaviors icon on any Launcher. The Behaviors panel opens.

3. In the Behaviors panel, click the add (+) action button.

4. From the pop-up menu, select the Timeline option and then select either Go to Timeline Frame, Play Timeline, or Stop Timeline.

5. In the dialog box that appears, select the name of the timeline you want to affect from the drop-down list. If you are working with the Go to Timeline Frame dialog box, you must also enter a frame number in the Go to Frame box and (if desired) enter a number in the Loop box. (Leaving the Loop box empty causes the animation to loop until the user closes the page.)

6. Click OK.

Dreamweaver adds and formats the behavior according to your selections and then updates the associated page code.

Part IX

Adding Multimedia Objects

In the Web's early days, designers could get away with presenting pages that contained only text and images. Now, however, both designers and users alike expect more dynamic sites. Just take a brief look at such sites as CNN (www.cnn.com) to understand and appreciate the power of adding video — streaming or downloadable — to your Web site. And for the talk-radio and music lovers among you, sites such as National Public Radio (www.npr.org) demonstrate how you can effectively use audio on your pages.

This part provides guidance to help you use Dreamweaver to incorporate both video and audio — as well as other multimedia objects, such as Java applets, Flash movies, and ActiveX controls — into your sites. Keep in mind that Dreamweaver can't help you build the multimedia elements themselves; it can only make existing multimedia objects accessible to users who view your page. (One notable exception is that Dreamweaver 4 does enable you to build Flash buttons and Flash text. *See also* Part VI for details.)

In this part . . .

Adding Audio

From music to sound effects to voice, you can use the Dreamweaver program to add virtually any genre of audio to your Web site. To do so, you must ensure that you save your audio in an acceptable Web format and store it in an accessible location.

You must save audio for the Web — regardless of how it's originally created — in a digital format prior to placing it online. Because audio files tend to be small, you can easily present audio in a downloadable format. Downloadable files require the user to wait for the file to completely transfer from the host to his computer before he can play the file. If you plan to use very long audio selections, you may instead choose to stream the selections. (*See also* "Streaming Audio and Video" later in this part.)

Acceptable Web audio formats

The following table lists Web audio formats that you can use along with the technologies users employ in playing back each format. The file extension of your audio filenames indicates the format in which you save the clip. For example, song.ra indicates a RealAudio clip. Numerous digital formats exist, and the audio format that you choose affects the technology that users employ when they play back your audio.

Audio File Format	Extensions	Common Use
AIFF	.aif, .aiff	Uncompressed files can be played in browsers but are slow to download.
Flash audio	.swf	Audio-only movies can stream PCM or MP3-compressed audio.
MIDI	.mid, .midi, .smf	Music files saved in the MIDI format. Plays in MIDI players (which are not well-standardized on the Web).
MP3	.mp3, .mp2	High-quality, compressed files with relatively speedy download times. Plays in numerous players, including QuickTime Player 4+, RealPlayer G2 6+, Windows Media Player 5.2+, and others that act as browser helper applications.
QuickTime	.mov	Soundtrack-only QuickTime movies. Plays in the QuickTime Player.

Audio File Format	Extensions	Common Use
RealAudio	.ra or .ram	Audio-only files in the RealMedia format. Plays in RealPlayer.
Rich Music Format	.rmf	Hybrid audio/music format. Plays in the Beatnik player.
Shockwave Audio	.swa	Audio-only Shockwave files that can be played by any MP3 player.
WAV	.wav	Uncompressed files can be played in browsers but are slow to download.
Windows Media	.asf, .asx	The Microsoft streaming media format. Plays in the Windows Media Player.

Embedding an audio file

One option for adding an audio file to your Web page is to build the sound directly into the page. This technique is useful if you want to make the details of the sound playback transparent to your page user. Users must have an appropriate plug-in for playing embedded audio of the format you use.

Embed an audio file by using the following steps:

1. In the Document window, click your page in the location where you want to add an embedded audio file.

2. Click the Insert Plugin button on the Special Objects panel or choose Insert⇨Media⇨Plugin from the Menu bar.

3. In the Select File dialog box that appears, enter the path to the audio file you want to embed and click the Select button. If the file is outside your current root directory, Dreamweaver asks whether you want to copy the file to your site root. Click Yes. Your audio file is embedded, and the Plugin Property Inspector appears. You can change the selected file in the Plugin Property inspector by typing a new name in the Src box or by browsing through the Src folder to select a file.

4. In the Plugin Property inspector, size the Audio Plugin place-holder to any dimensions you choose. You can either enter a width and height in the W and H text boxes in the Plugin Property inspector, or you can drag a handle on the place-holder to manually resize. A width of 144 pixels and a height of 60 pixels ensure that users can view all the audio playback controls in both Netscape Navigator and Internet Explorer.

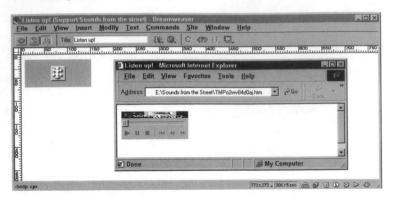

Dreamweaver embeds the audio file in your page and adds the associated code to the HTML.

 Click the Play button in the Plugin Property inspector to play your audio file without previewing your page in a browser.

Click the Parameters button in the Plugin Property inspector to open the Parameters dialog box, where you can precisely format the playback control console for your audio file.

 For users who do not have the plug-in, you can offer a link to a Web site where they can download the plug-in they need. In the Plg URL text box of the Plugin Property inspector, enter the URL where users can go to obtain the needed plug-in. Browsers not detecting the presence of the plug-in needed to play your clip direct users to this Web site.

Embedding background music

To cause background music to play after the user opens a page, follow these steps:

1. In the Document window, click anywhere on your Web page to add an embedded audio file.

 2. Click the Insert Plugin button on the Special Objects panel or choose Insert⇨Media⇨Plugin from the Menu bar.

3. In the Select File dialog box, enter the path to the audio file that you want to embed and click the Select button. If the file is outside your current root directory, Dreamweaver asks whether you want to copy the file to your site root. Click Yes. Your audio file is embedded, and the Plugin Property inspector appears. You can change the selected file in the Plugin Property inspector by typing a new name in the Src text box or by browsing in the Src folder to select a file.

4. In the Plugin Property inspector, enter a width and height of 2 in the W and H text boxes.

5. Click the Parameters button to open the Parameters dialog box.

6. In the Parameters dialog box, click the Add (+) button to add a new parameter.

7. Click in the Parameter column and type **hidden**. Then tab to the Value column and type **true**. This text hides the audio playback controls.

8. Click OK to complete the adding of parameters and close the dialog box.

To cause your background embedded audio clip to loop, include an additional parameter by typing **loop** in the Parameters dialog box. Give the loop parameter a value equal to the number of times that you want the clip to repeat. Or type **true** to make the clip loop until the user exits the page.

Linking to an audio file

A simple and relatively trouble-free way to include audio on a Web page is to link the page to an audio file. Users can select the link if they want to hear the clip. This selection opens a player outside the browser where the user can control audio playback.

To create a link to an audio file, select the text or image object that you want to set up as the link. Doing so opens the object's Property inspector. (If the inspector does not appear, open it by choosing Windows➪Properties from the Menu bar.) In the Link area of the Property inspector, enter the audio filename or browse to locate the audio file you want to link to. If the file is outside your current root directory, Dreamweaver asks whether you want to copy the file to your site root. Click Yes. Dreamweaver adds the link and updates your page code.

Adding Video

Video clips can add interest to your page by providing a television-like feel for the user. If you plan to use video, you must save your clip in a digital format prior to placing it online. Because videos tend to possess relatively large file sizes, they are most effective when they are kept very short. The shorter the clip, the less likely the user is to tire while waiting for the clip to download — and the less likely he or she is to surf to another page!

An alternative to using downloadable clips is to present the video in a streaming video format. The advantage of streaming your video is that users don't need to wait for the entire clip to download before having something to see and hear. (***See also*** "Streaming Audio and Video" later in this part.)

You can choose either to embed or link to video files, but you must take care to use a video format that's acceptable for Web playback.

Acceptable Web video formats

Following are the Web video formats you can use, along with the technologies users employ in playing back each format. The file extension of your video filename indicates the format in which you save the clip.

Video File Format	Extensions	Common Use
MPEG	`.mpg`, `.mpeg`, `.mpe`	High-quality, compressed files that play in Windows Media Player and on Macintosh via QuickTime.
QuickTime	`.mov`	QuickTime movies that play in the QuickTime Player on both Windows and Macintosh systems. Can include video and audio or just video-only.
RealAudio	`.ra` or `.ram`	Files in the RealMedia format. Plays in RealPlayer. Can include video and audio or just video-only.
Video for Windows	`.avi`	Once-popular format is becoming less prevalent but still plays in most players.

Embedding a video clip

Embedding a video file causes the file to play directly in the parent Web page. Users must have an appropriate plug-in for playing embedded video of the format you use. Embed video as follows:

1. In the Document window, click your page in the location where you want to add an embedded video file.

2. Click the Insert Plugin button on the Special Objects Panel or choose Insert⇨Media⇨Plugin from the Menu bar.

3. In the Select File dialog box, enter the path to the video file that you want to embed and click the Select button. If the file is outside your current root directory, Dreamweaver asks whether you want to copy the file to your site root. Click Yes. Your video file is embedded, and the Plugin Property inspector appears. You can change the selected file in the Plugin Property inspector by typing a new name in the Src text box or by browsing in the Src folder to select a file.

4. In the Plugin Property inspector, size the Video Plug-in placeholder to any dimensions you choose. Enter a width and height in the W and H boxes in the Plugin Property inspector or drag a handle on the placeholder to manually resize.

To play your video file without previewing your page in a browser, click the Play button in the Plugin Property inspector.

Use the Parameters dialog box to format the playback control console for your video file.

For users who do not have the plug-in for playing your embedded video, offer a link to a Web site where they can download the plug-in they need. In the Plg URL text box of the Plugin Property inspector, enter the URL where users can go to obtain the needed plug-in. Browsers not detecting the presence of the plug-in needed to play your clip will direct users to this Web site.

Linking to a video clip

You can use an image or text to create a link to a video clip. After the user clicks the link, the video opens and plays in a new window.

To create a link to a video file, select the text or image object that you want to set up as the link. Doing so opens the object's Property inspector. (If the inspector does not appear, open it by choosing Windows➪Properties from the Menu bar.) In the Link area of the Property inspector, enter the video filename or browse to locate the video file you want to link to. If the file is outside your current root directory, Dreamweaver asks whether you want to copy the file to your site root. Click Yes. Dreamweaver adds the link and updates your code.

Streaming Audio and Video

RealPlayer, from RealNetworks, Inc., offers you the capability to stream audio and video files for user playback. *Streaming* files begin playing as soon as a browser transfers sufficient information to the user's computer to stay ahead of the remaining portion of the file as it downloads. Streaming enables the user to experience your audio or video clip much sooner than with a downloadable file. This option is especially useful for large audio files and all but the shortest video files.

RealPlayer files have special names — specifically RealMedia — and may be further categorized as RealAudio or RealVideo. You must ensure that you save the audio and video you want to stream via RealPlayer in the RealMedia file format. You must also ensure that you create two additional files, called *metafiles*, to launch the RealPlayer media player.

RealMedia file formats

You must save RealMedia files using one of the filenames listed in the following table. Make sure that you create and save the RealPlayer metafiles as indicated.

RealMedia File Format	Extensions	Function
Audio, video, animation files	.rm, .ra, .rp, .rt, .swf	Media file saved in the format required for RealPlayer playback
Metafile for linked media	.ram	The file that launches the independent RealPlayer
Metafile for embedded media	.rpm	The file that launches the RealPlayer plug-in

Understanding how to create RealMedia metafiles and how to format RealMedia playback controls is no easy job. Alternatively, you can add RealMedia clips by using the RealSystem G2 Objects for Dreamweaver. The objects are available for free downloading at htttp://exchange.macromedia.com. Downloading these objects adds G2 Objects to your Objects panel, with buttons that enable you to more easily insert and format RealMedia in your Web pages.

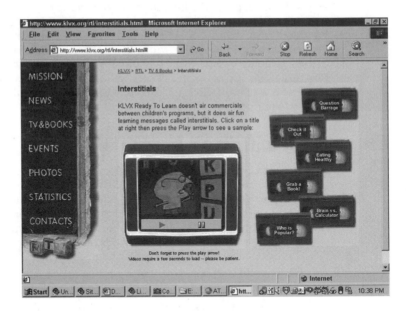

Embedding a RealMedia clip

Embedding a RealMedia clip causes the file to play directly in the parent Web page. Users must have the RealPlayer plug-in for playing embedded video of the format you use. Embed RealMedia by using the following steps:

1. In the Document window, click your page in the area that you want to add an embedded RealMedia file.

2. Click the Insert Plugin button on the Special Objects panel or choose Insert⇨Media Plugin from the Menu bar.

3. In the Select File dialog box, enter the path to the RealMedia file you want to embed and click the Select button. This .rpm metafile launches the RealPlayer plug-in (**See also** "RealMedia File Formats" in this part.) Your file is embedded, and the Plugin Property inspector appears. You can change the selected file in the Plugin Property inspector by typing a new name in the Src text box or by browsing in the Src folder to select a file.

4. In the Plugin Property inspector, size the RealMedia Plug-in placeholder to any dimensions you choose. Enter a width and height in the W and H text boxes in the Plugin Property inspector or drag a handle on the placeholder to manually resize.

5. Click the Parameters button to open the Parameters dialog box.

6. In the Parameters dialog box, click the Add (+) button to add a new parameter.

7. Click in the Parameter column, type **controls**, tab to the Value column, and then type **all**. Doing so shows the Image window where the RealMedia plays, along with the Control, Status, and Information panels.

8. Click OK to complete the adding of parameters and close the dialog box.

To play your RealMedia file without previewing your page in a browser, click the Play button in the Plugin Property inspector.

Use the Parameters dialog box to fine-tune the formatting of the playback control console for your RealMedia file.

For users who do not have the plug-in for playing your embedded RealMedia, offer a link to a Web site where they can download the plug-in they need. In the Plg URL box of the Plugin Property inspector, enter the URL where users can go to obtain the needed plug-in. Browsers not detecting the presence of the plug-in needed to play your clip direct users to this Web site. Direct users to www.realmedia.com to get the RealPlayer plug-in for a Real Audio clip on your page.

See the *Dreamweaver 3 Bible*, by Joseph W. Lowery (IDG Books Worldwide, Inc.), for helpful details on including RealMedia in your Web site.

Linking to a video clip

You can use an image or text to create a link to a RealMedia clip. When the user clicks the link, the clip opens and plays in a new window.

To create a link to a ReadMedia file, select the text or image object that you want to set up as the link. Doing so opens the object's Property inspector. (If the inspector does not show, open it by choosing Windows⇨Properties from the Menu bar.) In the Link area of the Property inspector, enter the RealMedia filename or browse to locate the file you want to link to. This file is the .ram file that launches the independent RealPlayer. (*See also* "RealMedia File Formats" earlier in this part.) Dreamweaver adds the link and updates your page code.

Using Other Media

Dreamweaver 4 enables you to easily insert a number of other multimedia formats into your Web pages, including ActiveX, Java Applets, Flash, and Shockwave. After inserting any of the following media, you can set the control and playback features of the media in the Parameters dialog box. Additionally, you can fine-tune the media action on your page by using the Behaviors panel to create triggering actions that cause the media to play, stop, and execute other functions. (*See also* Using Behaviors in Part VII.)

Follow these directions to insert other media:

1. In the Document window, click your page in the location where you want to add a multimedia file.

2. In the Objects panel, switch to the panel containing the button of the media type you want to use and then click that button. Or choose Insert⇨Media from the Menu bar and choose the media type that you want to use from the drop-down list.

Media type	Object Panel	Button
ActiveX	Special	
Applet	Special	
Flash	Common	
Shockwave	Common	

3. **For Applet, Flash, and Shockwave files:** In the Select File dialog box, enter the path to the media and click the Select button. Your file is attached, and the associated Property inspector appears. You can change the selected file in the Plugin Property inspector by typing a new name in the Src text box or by browsing in the Src folder to select a file.

For ActiveX: An ActiveX placeholder is inserted, and the
ActiveX Property inspector appears. Enter the name of the
ActiveX file you want to play in the Class ID text box.

4. In the Property inspector for your selected media, enter
dimensions in the W and H text boxes to size the Media placeholder to any dimensions you choose.

5. In the Property inspector for your selected media, click the
Parameters button to open the Parameter dialog box, where
you can format the playback of your media file.

See the reference materials for Flash and other multimedia programs for details on formatting and playing files on your Web pages
that you create with these programs.

Part X

Structuring Pages with Frames

Frames are divisions of a Web page that enable you to independently load information into distinct regions of your page. Frames are useful if you want to display certain information on-screen while changing other information. You frequently see three-frame pages on the Web — the top frame shows the site's title graphic; the left frame shows the navigation bar, and the large body frame changes to show whatever content you select.

A special HTML page called a *frameset* defines the structure and formatting of frames on your Web page. As you work with frames, be aware that you must always save the frameset page to lay out the size, position, and borders of your frames, along with the content that you want to display in each frame.

In this part . . .

Adding Frames

You can add a frame to a frameless Document window or to an existing frame within the Document window. Adding a frame to an existing frame divides the existing frame into two or more regions. The page describing the collective grouping of your frames is called a frameset.

Dreamweaver offers you the option of adding frames via the Menu bar or via the Frames Object panel.

Via the Menu bar

Click the Document window or existing frame in the area where you want to add a frame. Choose Insert⇨Frames and select an option from the drop-down list.

Frame Option	What It Does
Left	Creates a vertical frame down the left side
Right	Creates a vertical frame down the right side
Top	Creates a horizontal frame across the top
Bottom	Creates a horizontal frame across the bottom
Left and Top	Creates a square frame at the origin, a horizontal frame across the top, and a vertical frame down the left side
Left Top	Creates a vertical frame down the left side at the origin and a horizontal frame across the top
Top Left	Creates a horizontal frame across the top at the origin and a vertical frame down the left side
Split	Creates two frames of equal size and shape

Dreamweaver adds your frame and updates the associated HTML page code.

Via the Frames Objects panel

Click in the Document window or in an existing frame where you want to add a frame. Open the Frames Objects panel by choosing Window⇨Objects from the Menu bar and switching to Frames. Click a button at the Frames Objects panel corresponding to the frame type you want to create.

The light-blue frame in each button represents where the content of the existing frame is placed after you add the new frame.

Dreamweaver adds your frame and updates the associated HTML page code.

You can't add just one frame to a blank Document window. If you add one frame, you actually add two because the leftover area becomes a frame.

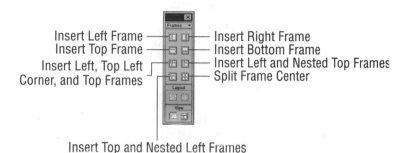

Insert Left Frame

Insert Top Frame

Insert Left, Top Left Corner, and Top Frames

Insert Right Frame

Insert Bottom Frame

Insert Left and Nested Top Frames

Split Frame Center

Insert Top and Nested Left Frames

Deleting Frames

To delete a frame, select the frame border and drag it to the edge of the parent frame or to the edge of the Document window — whichever is closer.

Dreamweaver deletes the selected frame and updates the associated HTML page code.

Formatting Frameset Borders

You can format the appearance of borders in your frameset by accessing the Frameset Property inspector. Just follow these steps:

1. Click a border of a frame in the frameset you want to modify.

Doing so opens the Frameset Properties inspector. If the inspector doesn't appear, open it by choosing Windows⇨Properties from the Menu bar.

2. In the Frameset Properties inspector, format the border appearance by selecting a choice from the Borders drop-down list box:

- **Yes:** Creates a three-dimensional look for the borders.

- **No:** Creates a single-color flat look for the borders.

- **Default:** Enables the user's browser to set how borders appear.

3. In the Frameset Properties inspector, enter a number in pixels in the Border Width text box.

The default is a border width of six pixels. If you don't want a border, enter zero.

4. In the Frameset Properties inspector, select a border color by clicking the Border Color swatch and selecting a color from the Color palette that appears.

Alternatively, you can enter a hexadecimal color code in the Border Color box.

Dreamweaver applies the modifications of your frameset borders and updates the associated HTML page code.

Moving between Frames in a Frameset

To select any frame in a frameset, simply click in that frame. If you have rulers turned on, the origin of the Document window resets to the origin of your selected frame. (**See also** Part I for details on working with rulers.)

Saving a Frame

Saving a frame means that you're saving the HTML page from which the source content of the frame originates. To save a frame, follow these steps:

1. Select the frame by clicking in it.

2. Choose File⇨Save Frame from the Menu bar.

3. On the first save, enter a name in the File Name text box of the Save As dialog box that appears and click Save.

Future saves require only that you complete Steps 1 and 2.

 You can save a frame as a different filename by selecting the frame and then choosing File⇨Save Frame As from the Menu bar. Then enter a new name in the File Name box.

Saving a Frameset

Saving a frameset means saving the layout of frame positions, frame names, and border formatting on a page. Keep in mind that you must still save individual frames to save the content contained in those frames. To save a frameset, follow these steps:

1. Select the frameset by clicking one of its borders.

2. Choose File⇨Save Frameset from the Menu bar.

3. On the first save, enter a name in the File Name text box of the Save As dialog box that appears and click Save.

Future saves require only that you complete Steps 1 and 2.

 If you also made changes to individual frames — not just the frameset — since your last save, Dreamweaver asks whether you want to save individual frames. Make sure that you do so.

 You can save a frameset as a different filename by selecting the frameset and then choosing File⇨Save Frameset As from the Menu bar. Then enter a new name in the File Name text box.

Setting Attributes of Individual Frames

You use the Frame Property inspector to select the source page that appears in a frame. You can also format the appearance of an individual frame in its Frame Property inspector. Individual frame settings override attributes previously assigned to the frame through frameset formatting. Format a frame by following these steps:

1. Open the Frames panel by choosing Window⇨Frames from the Menu bar.

   The Frames panel appears and displays a miniature version of the frameset for your entire page.

   Note: You can't simply click a frame to open its associated Frame Property inspector. If you click a frame, you're actually clicking the source page that resides in the frame — a process identical to clicking in the Document window for that page.

2. In the Frames panel, click the frame whose attributes you want to modify.

   The Frame Property inspector appears for the selected frame. If the inspector doesn't appear, open it by choosing Windows⇨Properties from the Menu bar.

3. In the Frame Property inspector, enter a name for your frame in the Frame Name text box.

   This name is the name by which the frame is referenced in the Frames panel, in Target drop-down lists, and in the HTML page code. The frame name must start with a letter, and you cannot use hyphens, spaces, or periods. You must also avoid using JavaScript reserved names, such as top.

4. In the Src text box, enter the name of the source page whose content you intend to display in the frame.

   Alternatively, you can click the Src folder and browse to select the source page.

5. Select a scrolling option for your selected frame from the Scroll drop-down menu. Options consist of:

   • **Yes:** Adds a scroll bar to the frame, whether it's needed or not.

   • **No:** Doesn't add a scroll bar to the frame, even if needed.

   • **Auto:** Places a scroll bar in the frame if the frame contents exceed the frame boundaries.

   • **Default:** Places a scroll bar in the frame depending on the user's browser settings.

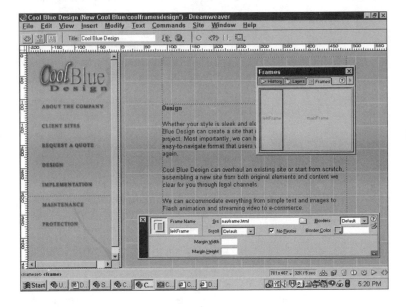

6. Click to check the No Resize check box if you don't want the user to be able to resize the frame.

   If you do want the user to be able to resize the frame, leave the check box unchecked.

7. Format the frame border appearance by selecting a choice from the Borders drop-down list box:

- **Yes:** Creates a three-dimensional look for the borders.

- **No:** Creates a single-color flat look for the borders.

- **Default:** Enables the user's browser to set how borders appear.

8. Select a border color for the frame by clicking the Border Color swatch and selecting a color from the Color palette that appears.

   Alternatively, you can enter a hexadecimal color code in the Border Color text box.

9. Enter a number in pixels in the Margin Width and the Margin Height text boxes.

   Margin Width specifies the horizontal standoff space between the frame content and the frame border. Margin Height specifies the vertical standoff space between the frame content and the frame border.

Dreamweaver applies your frame settings and updates the associated HTML page code.

Choosing No Resize in the Frame Property inspector doesn't prevent you, the designer, from resizing the frame in the Document window — it just prevents page users from resizing the frame in their browsers.

Don't overlook completing the Frame Name text box. Naming your frame is a vital step in completing frame-targeting assignments. (*See also* "Targeting Content" later in this part.)

Setting No Frames Content

Text-based browsers and many older browsers frequently don't support frames and can't correctly display pages that you create by using frames.

To help ensure that the maximum number of users can view your page correctly, Dreamweaver offers you a method for building *no-frames* pages as companions to your frame-enabled pages. To create a no-frames page for your current frameset, follow these steps:

1. Choose Modify⇔Frameset⇔Edit NoFrames Content from the Menu bar.

   A blank, NoFrames Content page appears in the Document window and replaces your frame-enabled page.

2. On the NoFrames Content page, insert the information that you want to appear in No Frames browsers.

3. Return to your frame-enabled page by choosing Modify➪ Frameset➪Edit NoFrames Content from the Menu bar.

Dreamweaver includes your No Frames content in the associated HTML page code.

Sizing and Resizing Frames

Dreamweaver enables you to adjust the width and the height of any frame that you create. You can make your adjustments in either the Document window or in the Frameset Property inspector.

Via the Document window

Click the column or row border that you want to adjust. Drag it to create new frame dimensions. The dimensions of your modified frames are reflected in the Frameset Property inspector.

Via the Frameset Property inspector

To modify frame dimensions, follow these steps:

1. Click a border of the frame that you want to adjust.

   Doing so opens the Frameset Property inspector. (If the inspector doesn't show, choose Windows➪Properties from the Menu bar to open the inspector.)

2. In the RowCol selection box of the Frameset Property inspector, click the thumbnail frame representing the frame that you want to adjust.

   The selected frame appears shaded, and the attributes of your selection appear in the inspector.

3. In the Row or Column Value text box, enter a number for the size of your selected frame and select the Units for your frame size from the drop-down list.

   A Row Value specifies the frame height, and a Column Value specifies the frame width. You can choose pixels, percentage, or relative as follows:

   • **Pixels:** Sets the frame height or width to the exact number of pixels that you enter in the Value text box.

   • **Percentage:** Sets the frame height or width to a percentage of the screen size. The number that you enter in the Value text box must be between 1 and 100.

- **Relative:** Sets the frame height or width to a size relative to the other frames. Leave the Value text box blank to make a relative- sized frame fill the remainder of the screen. Or enter a scale factor such as 2 or 3 to make the frame that many times larger than another relative frame.

Dreamweaver modifies your frame and updates the associated HTML page code.

Targeting Content

The advantage of constructing Web pages with frames is that you can display several HTML pages at the same time, and you can selectively *target* content by specifying which frame you want to display an HTML page.

For example, you can set up a two-frame frameset in which you use the left frame for navigation and you use the main frame to display any link the user clicks in the navigation frame. You need only set up the link to target the main frame as the location where you want the selected HTML page to open.

Set up a target by following these steps:

1. Select the text or image that you want to act as a link.

   Doing so opens the associated Property inspector. If the inspector doesn't appear, open it by choosing Windows⇨ Properties from the Menu bar.

2. In the Link box, enter the name of the HTML source page whose content is to appear in the frame. Alternatively, you can click the Link folder and browse to select the source page.

3. From the Target drop-down menu, select the target frame where the link is to appear. All available targets are listed in the menu. These targets include the names of all frames you set up and also the following system-wide targets:

   - **_blank:** Opens a new browser window and shows the link in that window. The current window remains open.

   - **_parent:** Opens the link in a window that replaces the frameset containing the current page.

- **_self:** Opens the link in the current frame. The linked page replaces the page in the current frame. This setting is the default target.

- **_top:** Opens the link in a window that replaces the outermost frameset of the current page. (Same as _parent, unless you're using nested framesets.)

Dreamweaver creates your target and updates the associated HTML page code.

 After saving pages where you create targets, always preview your work in a browser to ensure that your links open the correct HTML page in the intended frame. To preview your page, choose File⇨ Preview in Browser from the Menu bar or click the Preview in Browser button.

Part XI

Incorporating Forms

Forms on the Web serve the same purpose as the paper-based forms you fill out — they provide a structured format for gathering specific information. The difference is that Web-based forms usually require less time for keyboard-savvy users to fill out (and using Web-based forms also saves a few trees otherwise destined for a paper mill).

Dreamweaver offers you a number of handy tools for creating Web-based forms that you can easily include on your Web pages. You can incorporate everything from text boxes to radio buttons, and you can create surveys, gather user data, and conduct e-commerce.

In this part . . .

Adding a Form

Before you can insert specific form objects — such as check boxes — on your Web page, you must first add a form to the page so that the appropriate code is written to the HTML page code. You can add a form directly to the Document window, or in a table cell or in a layer.

 To add a form to a page, click in the Document window where you want to add the form and then choose Insert⇨Form from the Menu bar or click the Insert Form button on the Forms Objects panel. If the Forms Objects panel is not open, choose Window⇨Objects from the Menu bar to open the panel.

Dreamweaver adds the form to the page as indicated by the red dashed lines, and also adds the associated form tag to your HTML page code.

You can now insert form objects between the red dashed lines of the form.

 If you attempt to add a form object without first adding a form, a dialog box appears, asking whether you want to add a form tag. Click the Yes button to add both the form tag and the object to your page. Click the No button to add the form object without adding the form.

Building Drop-Down Menus

Drop-down lists present a list of choices from which the form user can make a selection. You can include as many choices as you want in the list, but only one choice shows on-screen until the user clicks the drop-down list to see the other choices. The user can select only a single item from the list of choices. When the user makes a choice, that selection becomes the item that shows on-screen.

 To insert a drop-down list, position the cursor in the area of the Document window where you want to add the list and choose Insert⇨Form Objects⇨List/Menu Button from the Menu bar or click the Insert List/Menu button on the Form Objects panel. If the Form Objects panel is not open, choose Window⇨Objects from the Menu bar to open the panel.

Dreamweaver adds the drop-down list to your form, and a List/Menu Property inspector appears. If the Property inspector does not show, open it by choosing Window⇨Properties from the Menu bar.

Fill in the following fields of the List/Menu Property inspector to format the drop-down list:

- ✔ **List/Menu name:** Enter a name in the empty box.

- ✔ **Type:** Leave the <u>M</u>enu radio button selected.

- ✔ **List Values:** Click this button to open the List Values dialog box where you can add, remove, and modify items on your list. (***See also*** "Working with List Values" later in this part.) Click OK to apply your additions or edits and close the dialog box.

- ✔ **Initially Selected:** Click the item in the list that the user sees on first encountering the drop-down list. (***Note:*** You must click the expander button in the bottom-right corner of the Property inspector to view this formatting option.)

Dreamweaver adds the code for the drop-down list and the associated formatting to the HTML for the page.

The drop-down list is identical conceptually to a group of radio buttons. The drop-down list, however, saves space because it expands to show all choices only if the user is making a selection.

Constructing a Jump Menu

A *jump menu* is a tool that offers users a list of pages that they can jump to on your site. Although jump menus are really used for navigational purposes, you create jump menus by using form objects and set them up by using procedures similar to those for setting up other form objects.

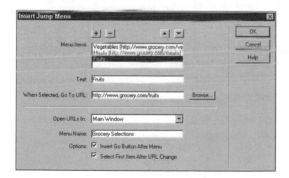

To insert a jump menu, follow these steps:

1. In the Document window, position the cursor where you want to add the menu and choose <u>I</u>nsert⇨Form O<u>b</u>jects⇨<u>J</u>ump Menu from the Menu bar or click the Insert Jump Menu button on the Form Objects panel. If the Form Objects panel is not open, choose Window⇨Objects from the Menu bar to open the panel.

2. In the Insert Jump Menu dialog box that appears, go to the Text text box and enter the name of the first list item for your menu.

3. In the When Selected, Go to URL text box, enter the page or address of the page where you want the current list item to jump. Alternatively, you can click the Browse button and choose a file from the Select File dialog box that appears.

4. Add additional jump menu items by clicking the + button and repeating Steps 2 and 3.

5. From the Open URLs In drop-down list, select the destination target where the user sees his selected jump page open. If you are working with a frameset, all frames appear in the list as options for the target. (*See also* Part X for details on targeting frames in a frameset.) Otherwise, only Main Window appears.

6. Enter a name for your jump menu in the Menu Name text box.

7. If you want, click to check the Options check boxes as follows:

   Insert Go Button After Menu: Selecting this option causes your jump menu to delay jumping until the user clicks the Go button.

   Select First Item After URL Change: Selecting this option causes the jump menu to reset to the top of the list following a jump.

8. Click the OK button to apply your selections and close the dialog box.

Dreamweaver adds the jump menu to the Document window and the associated code to the HTML for the page.

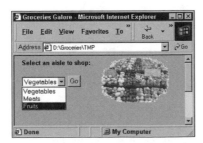

You can remove any jump menu item in the Insert Jump Menu dialog box by selecting the item in the Menu Items list and clicking the remove (–) button. Edit any item by selecting it in the Menu Items list and by typing new information in the text boxes.

Resequence a jump menu in the Insert Jump Menu dialog box by clicking an item and then clicking the down or up button to move the item lower or higher in the list.

Create a null jump menu item — for example, a title for the list of items, such as "Choose Your Beanie Baby" — by entering a # sign in the When Selected, Go to URL text box.

Creating Scrolling Lists

A *scrolling list* presents a list of choices from which the form user can make a selection. You can include as many choices as you want in the actual list, and you can choose how many items appear on-screen in the list, an attribute called the *list height*. A user can click the up or down scroll button to see other choices in the list but can never see the entire list at once. The height you set limits the user's choices. You can opt to have the user select only one choice or multiple choices. After the user makes a choice, that item becomes selected (highlighted) in the list.

To insert a scrolling list, position the cursor in the Document window where you want to add the scrolling list and choose Insert⇨Form Objects⇨List/Menu Button from the Menu bar or click the Insert List/Menu button on the Form Objects panel. If the Form Objects panel is not open, choose Window⇨Objects from the Menu bar to open the panel.

Dreamweaver adds a list to your form, and a List/Menu Property inspector appears. The list Type is initially Menu — you must change it to List. If the Property inspector does not appear, open it by choosing Window⇨Properties from the Menu bar.

Fill in the following options of the List/Menu Property inspector to format the scrolling list:

- **List/Menu name:** Enter a name in the empty text box.

- **Type:** Select the List radio button.

- **Height:** Enter a number to indicate how many list items you want to appear on-screen.

- **Selections:** Click the check box to Allow Multiple if you want the user to be able to select more than one list item. You must inform users that, if they want to select multiple items, they must press and hold the Ctrl key (Windows) or Cmd key (Macintosh) while clicking each item.

✔ **List Values:** Click this button to open the List Values dialog box, where you can add, remove, and modify items on your list. (*See also* "Working with List Values" later in this part.) Click OK to apply your additions or edits and close the dialog box.

✔ **Initially Selected:** Click a list item that the user sees on first encountering the scrolling list. To select multiple items, press and hold the Ctrl key (Windows) or Cmd key (Macintosh) as you click each item. (*Note:* You must click the Expander button in the bottom-right corner of the Property inspector to view this formatting option.)

Dreamweaver adds the code for the scrolling list and its associated formatting to the HTML for the page.

The scrolling list is a space-saving way to build a form object that's conceptually identical to a group of check boxes.

Editing Form Objects

To edit any form object, simply double-click the object in the Document window. Doing so opens the dialog box or Property inspector in which you originally set up the object. You can make your edits by adding, deleting, or changing information in the dialog box or Property inspector by using the same techniques that you use during setup.

Inserting Check Boxes

Providing a person using your form with check boxes enables the user to select as many of the items listed as applicable. The user simply clicks the check box to select the item and clicks again to deselect the item.

To insert a check box, position the cursor in the Document window where you want to add the check box and choose Insert➪Form Objects➪Check box from the Menu bar or click the Insert Check box button on the Form Objects panel. If the Form Objects panel is not open, choose Window➪Objects from the Menu bar.

A check box is added to your form, and a Check box Property inspector appears. If the Check box Property inspector does not appear, choose Window➪Properties from the Menu bar to open the Check box Property inspector.

Fill in the following options of the Check box Property inspector to format the check box:

- ✔ **Check box name:** Enter a name in the empty box or accept the default name assigned by Dreamweaver. Naming the check box is not mandatory.

- ✔ **Checked Value:** Enter a name in this text box for the item that the form user is selecting.

- ✔ **Initial State:** Click a radio button to indicate whether the box appears Checked or Unchecked when the user first sees it.

Dreamweaver adds the code for the check box and its associated formatting to the HTML for the page.

Inserting Radio Buttons

Radio buttons present the form user with a list of items from which the user can select only a single item. The user simply clicks the radio button to select the item. Users can click a different button on the form to change their selection. Doing so deselects the user's first choice because the user can select only one radio button in a group.

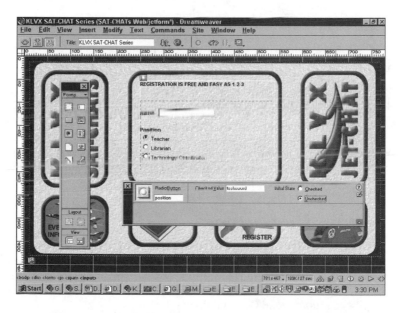

 To insert a radio button, click where you want to add the radio button in the Document window and choose Insert⇨Form Objects⇨Radio Button from the Menu bar or click the Insert radio button on the Form Objects panel. If the Form Objects panel is not open, choose Window⇨Objects from the Menu bar to open the panel.

A radio button is added to your form, and a Radio Button Property inspector appears. If the Radio Button Property inspector does not appear, choose Window⇨Properties from the Menu bar to open the inspector.

Fill in the following options of the Radio Button Property inspector to format the radio button:

✔ **RadioButton name:** Enter a name in the empty text box. All radio buttons in a group must have the same name.

✔ **Checked Value:** Enter a name in this text box for the item that the form user is selecting.

✔ **Initial State:** Click a radio button to indicate whether the box appears Checked or Unchecked when the user first sees it. You can check only one radio button in a group.

Dreamweaver adds the code for the radio button and the radio button's associated formatting to the HTML code for the page.

Labeling Form Objects

Dreamweaver enables you to provide labels for form objects and provide the user with directions about how to complete the information requested for each option. To label form objects, simply position your cursor in the form and begin typing. Then insert the form object you want.

You can also enter text following an inserted form object. Doing so may prove helpful in requesting multiple pieces of data with different units, such as a height in feet and inches. You can follow the first textbox or drop-down list with the text **feet** and the second with the text **inches**.

Setting Up Buttons

After a user enters data into a form, the user must then perform some sort of task to transmit the data from his computer to another computer that can process the information. Dreamweaver offers you three buttons to use to activate your form: Reset, Submit, and Command, as follows:

✔ **Reset:** After the user clicks this button, it erases all data entered into the form.

✓ **Submit:** After the user clicks this button, it sends all entered form data to the specified Action — which indicates whether the data is passed to a processing program or goes to a mailto: address.

✓ **Command:** After the user clicks this button, it executes whatever programming function the Web designer assigns to it.

To insert a button, click where you want to add the button in the Document window and choose Insert⇨Form Objects⇨Button from the Menu bar or click the Insert Button on the Form Objects panel. If the Objects panel is not open, choose Window⇨Objects from the Menu bar.

Dreamweaver adds a button to your form, and a Button Property inspector appears. If the Button Property inspector does not appear, choose Window⇨Properties from the Menu bar to open the inspector.

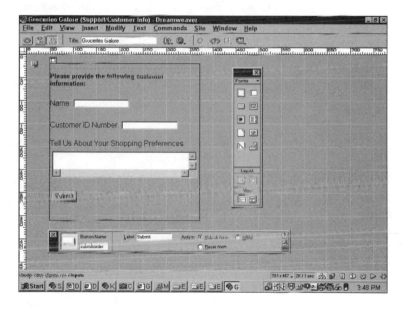

Fill in the following fields of the Button Property inspector to format the button:

✓ **Button name:** Enter a name in the empty text box. This name identifies the button in the HTML code.

✓ **Label:** Enter a name for the button to appear on-screen.

✓ **Action:** Click a radio button to indicate the function of the button. Choices consist of Reset form, Submit form, and None (Command).

Dreamweaver adds the code for the button and its associated formatting to the HTML for the page.

 You can create a graphical Submit button — a button created from a small image — by choosing Insert➪Form Objects➪Image Field from the Menu bar or by clicking the Insert Image Field button on the Form Objects panel.

Specifying Form Properties

A form possesses three properties that you can set at the Form Property inspector: Form Name, Action, and Method. Click the form to open the Form Property inspector. If the Property inspector does not appear, open it by choosing Window➪Properties from the Menu bar. Then specify the following properties:

✔ **Form Name:** Enter an alphanumeric name in the empty text box. The advantage of naming your form is that you can use the name to reference the form in a scripting language that you use to retrieve, store, and manipulate the form data.

✔ **Action:** Enter the address of the location that processes the form data. Alternatively, you can browse to the location by clicking the folder and making a selection at the Select File dialog box.

You may select the following three common actions:

• Enter the URL of a Common Gateway Interface (CGI) program that runs after the user submits the form. The action resembles the following:

```
www.server.com/cgi-bin/formhandler.pl
```

• Enter the JavaScript program that runs after the user submits the form. The action appears as follows:

```
www.server.com/javascript:function()
```

Here, `function` is your form handling function.

• Enter a mailto: address where the form data goes after the user clicks Submit. A mailto: address appears similar to the following:

```
mailto:gruntworker@formhandling.com
```

✔ **Method:** Select a method from the drop-down list for how the form data passes to the processing entity that specifies in the Action. Choices are Default, GET, and POST. (Default and GET are the same.) GET sends the form data by appending it to the URL that the Action specifies. POST sends the form data as a separate entity. GET limits the amount of data that can pass along, but POST does not.

If using mailto: addresses, be aware that the user's browser must be configured to send e-mail — otherwise, the user is unable to submit the form. Also be aware that the data received at the specified mailto: address is not formatted for easy reading: It appears as strings of code with the form data embedded within lots of ampersands and plus signs.

Using Text Fields

Text fields are blank text boxes that you can insert in your form to hold alphanumeric information that the user types. You can set up a text field to hold a single line of text, multiple lines of text, or a password as follows:

✓ **Single line:** Provides space for the user to enter a single word or short phrase of text.

✓ **Multi line:** Provides space for the user to enter a longer string of text. Appropriate for a comment box.

✓ **Password:** Provides space for the user to enter a password. An asterisk (Windows) or dot (Macintosh) appears on-screen for each character that the user types.

To add a text field: In the Document window, click where you want to add the radio button and choose Insert➪Form Objects➪Text Field from the Menu bar or click the Insert Text Field button on the Form Objects panel. If the Form Objects panel is not open, choose Window➪Objects from the Menu bar to open the panel.

Dreamweaver adds a text field to your form, and a Text Field Property inspector appears. If the Text Field Property inspector does not appear, choose Window➪Properties from the Menu bar to open the inspector.

Fill in the following fields of the Text Field Property inspector to format the text field:

✓ **TextField name:** Enter a name in the empty box. The field is referenced by this name in the HTML page code.

✓ **Char Width:** Enter a whole number for the approximate visible width of the field. (The width is approximate because text characters in your form are displayed differently according to users' browser settings.)

✓ **Max Chars** (applies to Single line and Password only): Enter a whole number to indicate the maximum number of characters the user can enter in the field. Max Chars can be equal to or greater than Char Width.

✔ **Num Lines** (applies to Multi line only): Enter a whole number for the maximum number of lines the user can enter in the field.

✔ **Type:** Click a radio button for Single line, Multi line, or Password.

✔ **Init Val:** (Optional) Enter an alphanumeric word or phrase that occupies the text field when the user first encounters the field. The user can enter his own information over the Init Val.

✔ **Wrap** (applies to Multi line only): Select an option for text wrapping from the drop-down list. Options consist of Default, Off, Virtual, or Physical. Default and Off are the same and do not wrap text until the user clicks the Enter (Windows) or Return (Macintosh) key. TheVirtual option wraps text on the user's screen but not when the form is submitted. The Physical option wraps text both on the user's screen and when the form is submitted.

Dreamweaver adds the code for the text field and its associated formatting to the HTML for the page.

Working with List Values

The List Values dialog box enables you to set the names and other attributes of items you present to a user in a form object. In a List Values dialog box, you can perform the following tasks:

✔ Click the add (+) button to add a new item to the list. Remove an item by clicking that item and clicking the remove (–) sign.

✔ Enter the name for the new item in the Item Label list.

✔ Enter the value for each item in the Value list. After the user submits the form, the value for each list item passes to the processing application you set in the Action. (**See also** "Specifying Form Properties" earlier in this part.) For items without values, the item labels pass along instead.

✔ Resequence the list by clicking an item and then clicking the down or up arrow to move the item lower or higher in the list.

Mapping Your Entire Site

Web pages you assemble in Dreamweaver are more than just standalone files composed of text and pretty images. Your pages are pieces of a larger whole, presented together to create an entire site and linked so that users can navigate around in whatever order best suits their needs. Dreamweaver also gives you choices for the addressing that you can use for constructing the links, which connect your pages to each other and to other documents on the Web.

To assist you in setting up your overall site, Dreamweaver offers a number of tools to assemble your individual pages into a cohesive whole. Dreamweaver also offers a choice of views, where you can either look at your pages in a list format, where files are listed by name and grouped by folder, or in a mapped format, where files are presented visually as a map showing the relationship among your pages. This part covers all the tools and views you need to *set your sites*.

In this part . . .

Addressing Links

Addressing links in a Web site is similar to addressing envelopes for delivery via the US Postal Service. You must not only specify your destination address, but you must format the address using a structure that's understood by the delivery system.

Decide on the type of addressing that you want to use prior to creating any Web pages. Doing so helps you maintain an organized approach to designing how the pages work together within your site. Any of three address formats are available for links you set up in your site: absolute addresses, document-relative addresses, or site root-relative addresses. (*See also* "Absolute addresses," "Document-relative addresses," and "Site root-relative addresses" in this part for details.)

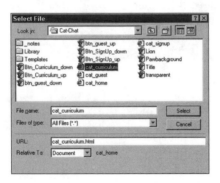

When you create a new link or edit a link on a page, you must indicate which of these formats you want to use in the Select File dialog box. In the Select File dialog box, you can do one of the following:

- ✔ Enter an absolute address in the URL text box.

- ✔ Select an HTML file from your documents and choose either Document or Site Root from the Relative To drop-down list.

You can create a new link by selecting the object you want to serve as a link and choosing Modify⇨Make Link from the Menu bar. Then indicate your link in the Select File dialog box. You can change an existing link by selecting the link and choosing Modify⇨Change Link from the Menu bar and then making your change in the Select File dialog box.

Absolute addresses

When you set up a link using an *absolute address,* you are defining the exact Uniform Resource Locator (URL) on the Web. No matter where the document is located that references an absolute address, the absolute address is the same for all pages that link to that document from anywhere on the Web.

A URL can have up to six different parts, although you often see URLs using fewer than all six. Slashes, colons, or some combination of the two usually separates the parts. A URL possessing all possible parts is structured as follows:

```
method://server:port/path/file#anchor
```

Most URLs end up using only a subset of all possible parts and look something like this:

```
www.coolbluedesign.com/index.htm
```

You want to use absolute addresses only when you want to link to pages outside your own site.

Document-relative addresses

Document-relative addresses don't require you to include the method, server, or path parts of the address. This type of address requires you to identify where the link file is located relative to the current document, as follows:

- ✔ If the link file is in the same folder as the current document, you need only to select the filename from the files that appear in the Select File dialog box. Or just enter the name in the File Name text box of the Select Files dialog box.

  For example, the filename may resemble aboutus.html.

- ✔ If the link file is located in a subfolder of the current document, enter the folder name followed by a forward slash followed by the filename in the File Name text box of the Select Files dialog box.

  For example, the filename may resemble company/aboutus.html.

  Each forward slash indicates that the file is contained in another subfolder of organization.

✔ If the link file is located in a folder above the current document, enter two dots followed by the filename and then a forward slash in the File Name text box of the Select Files.

For example, the filename may resemble ./aboutus.html.

Each set of two dots and a forward slash indicates that the file is contained in another folder up in the organization.

Site root-relative addresses

A *site root-relative address* indicates where the link file is located relative to the primary directory of the current site. Site root-relative addresses don't require you to include the method and server parts of the address — but they do require you to include the path. To name a site root-relative address, enter a forward slash followed by the folder name and then another forward slash followed by the filename in the File Name text box of the Select Files dialog box.

For example, the filename may resemble /company/aboutus.html.

Each forward slash indicates that the file is located another folder up in the organization of your files.

Checking Links Sitewide

Dreamweaver provides you with the ability to check all of the links within your site to help you troubleshoot whether your navigation structures are operating as you intend. You can check links from anywhere in Dreamweaver — in the Document window, in Site Files View, or in Map View.

Follow these steps to check the links within a site:

1. In any view, choose Site⇨Check Links Sitewide from the Menu bar.

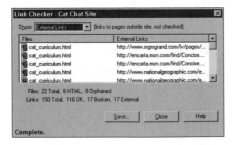

2. In the Link Checker dialog box, select from the S<u>h</u>ow drop-down list the type of link you want check. Your choices are:

- **Broken Links:** Links to files that are not found on your local system

- **External Links:** Links to pages outside the site (usually absolute addresses) that are not checked

- **Orphaned Files:** Web pages or other files (such as images) that do not link with any other file in your site

3. Click <u>S</u>ave if you want to save a record of the Sitewide Link check for future reference. Then enter a filename in the Save As dialog box and click the <u>S</u>ave button.

4. Click <u>C</u>lose to close the dialog box.

After constructing your site and putting it on the Web, make sure that you frequently check that any absolute address links you set up still work as you want them to. If you do need to update a link sitewide, you can do so by using the Change Link Sitewide feature. (**See also** Part XIV for more on the Change Link Sitewide feature.)

Creating Design Notes

Design notes are comments that you — or anyone else working on your site — can attach to your pages. Design notes serve as a sort of Dreamweaver sticky notepad and cannot be viewed by users examining your site in a browser. Web designers collaborating on a site find these notes useful for keeping track of which work has been finished and which activities remain to be completed.

Enabling design notes

Enable the design notes feature as follows:

1. **For a new site:** In any view, choose Site⇨New Site from the Menu bar.

   For the current site: Switch to the Site window. In the Site Name text box, double-click the drop-down arrow. Doing so opens the Site Definition dialog box.

2. Select the Design Notes category.

3. Enable design notes by clicking the <u>M</u>aintain Design Notes check box.

4. Click the Upload Design Notes for Sharing if you want other designers that you collaborate with to view your design notes for this site.

5. Click OK to close the Site Definition dialog box or choose another category to define.

Click the Clean Up button to remove old design notes at the end of a project before uploading the site to a host.

Attaching design notes

You can add design notes to a page in the Document window, in Site Files View, or in Map View. Include design notes for a page, as follows:

1. In any view, right-click (Windows) or Control-click (Macintosh) anywhere on the page to attach a note.

2. Select Design Notes for Page from the menu to open the Design Notes dialog box.

   Note: In Site Files View and Map View, select Design Notes.

Date icon

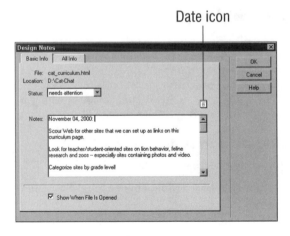

3. Click the Date icon to insert the current date.

4. In the Basic Info tab, enter any information you want in the Notes area.

5. In the Status drop-down box, select a status for your notes from the following choices: none, draft, revision1, revision2, revision3, alpha, beta, final, and needs attention.

6. Click to select the Show When File Is Opened check box if you want the design notes to show when you or a collaborator open the page in Dreamweaver.

7. Click OK to save your design notes and close the dialog box.

You can make edits to the way design notes are coded in the HTML page code in the All Info tab of the Design Notes dialog box.

Defining a Local Site

The *local site root* is the set of files on your computer that you create and assemble to build a Web site. You define the local site at the very beginning of any new development project. Ultimately, you store every HTML code page, image, video, sound — and any other Web files you use in your site — in the local site root. Eventually, you transfer a copy of your entire local site root to a folder on the Web server that hosts your site. (For details on working with the host server for your site, *see also* Part XIV.)

Set up a local site root as follows:

1. On your computer, create and name a new folder.

2. In Dreamweaver, choose Site⇨New Site from the Menu bar. Doing so opens the Site Definition dialog box.

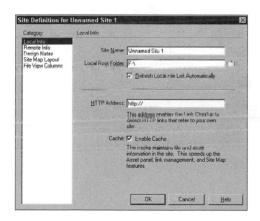

3. Select the Local Info category.

4. Enter a name in the Site Name text box. The site name you assign is for your reference and does not appear on any Web pages.

5. In the Local Info area, browse to locate the folder you created in Step 1. Doing so assigns that folder as the Local Root Folder for your site — the folder containing all of your HTML documents (Web pages) and dependent files (such as images).

6. Keep the Refresh Local File Lists Automatically check box checked. Doing so causes new files to be added to your file list automatically.

7. Click OK to close the dialog box or choose another category to define.

You don't need to complete the other areas of the Local Info category until you are ready to transfer your local site to the host site.

Edit the site definition of a site that you already created by choosing Site⇨Define Sites from the Menu bar. In the Define Sites dialog box, select the site you want to edit and click the Edit button. Doing so opens the Site Definition dialog box, where you can make your edits.

Laying Out the Site Map

Dreamweaver enables you to format certain attributes regarding exactly how the Site Map is displayed. Follow this procedure to edit how Dreamweaver lays out the Site Map in your current site:

1. In Dreamweaver, switch to the Site window. In the Site Name text box, double-click the drop-down arrow.

Doing so opens the Site Definition dialog box.

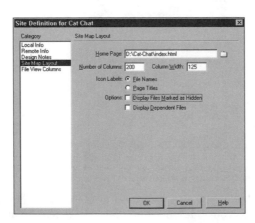

2. Select the Site Map Layout category.

3. Enter a name for your Home Page or click the folder to browse for an existing document. In the Site Map, your home page displays as the topmost document in the hierarchy of your site. Most people name their home pages using index.htm or index.html.

4. In the Number of Columns text box, enter a number for the number of columns your Site Map can display horizontally. The larger the number, the more horizontal scrolling you perform. The smaller the number, the more vertical scrolling you perform.

5. In the Icon Labels radio button, select to view documents in the site map either by File Names or Page Titles.

6. In the Options check boxes, make either of these choices:

   • **Display Files Marked As Hidden:** Causes the Site Map to show hidden documents and their dependent files. These filenames are formatted in italics.

   • **Display Dependent Files:** Causes images and other non-HTML documents to appear in the Site Map.

7. Click OK to close the dialog box or choose another category to define.

Looking at Site Files

Dreamweaver enables you to format the appearance of the site files in your current site as follows:

1. In Dreamweaver, switch to the Site window. In the Site Name text box, double-click the drop-down arrow. Doing so opens the Site Definition dialog box.

2. Select the File View Columns category.

3. Select a Column Name and then make the following choices:

   • **Align Checkbox:** Select Left, Center, or Right from the drop-down menu depending on how you want column content aligned in the Site Files.

   • **Options: Show Checkbox:** Click to check or uncheck this check box depending on whether you want the selected column to show in your Site Files.

4. Reorder column names by clicking a name and clicking the up- or down-arrow button in the dialog box to adjust position in the list.

5. If you want, select the Enable Column Sharing check box so that longer filenames can spill over into neighboring columns.

6. Click OK to close the dialog box.

Add a new column by clicking the add (+) button and entering a name in the Column Name text box. Select an option from the Associate with Design Note drop-down list. Options consist of Assigned, Due, Priority, and Status. The column type of your new column is labeled Personal in the Site Files.

Viewing Your Site

You have several options for viewing and manipulating your site as a whole.

Site Files View

Site Files View is simply a list of all the HTML documents and dependent files contained in your site, grouped by folder. Dreamweaver presents these files with information about each file contained in columns. Six built-in column names exist (Name, Notes, Size, Type, Modified, and Checked Out By), but you can add and name new columns as needed.

To examine your site in Site Files View, switch to the Site window and then click the Site Files View button. Site files appear in the right pane of your Site window. Alternatively, you can choose Window⇨Site Files from the Menu bar.

You can manage files in this view in a similar fashion to managing files in any Windows file system. For example, you can open any document by double-clicking it, and you can move documents between folders by dragging and dropping the documents as needed.

Adjust the size of the Site Files pane by dragging its window frame. For details on adjusting other attributes of how your site files appear in Site Files View, *see also* "Looking at Site Files" earlier in this part.

Site Map View

Dreamweaver offers a handy view for examining your site visually — the Site Map View. When working with the Site Map, a document icon represents each of your Web pages. Your site home page is displayed in the top of the map structure. Lines connecting the document icons show the relationship between Web pages in the site. Links and dependent files are listed below their associated document icons.

 To view your site as a map only, switch to the Site window. Click and hold down the Site Map View button and choose Map Only from the pop-up menu. Your Site Map appears full screen.

Any page possessing its own links is labeled with a small plus (+) sign. You can click the + sign to expand your view of the page to show all of its included links. Click the minus (–) sign on an expanded page to return the page to a collapsed view.

Links to other pages in your site root display in black. Links to absolute address URLs and e-mail addresses are display in blue. Links to pages that do not exist (for example, deleted pages, mis-named pages, or pages not yet created) are considered broken links and display in red. (These pages also show a broken link icon.)

See also "Laying Out the Site Map," earlier in this part, for details on adjusting how your Site Map appears in Site Map View.

 The home page icon usually appears in the top of the Site Map hier-archy, but you can change the icon's location so that you can view the map from the perspective of any page in your site. In the Site Map pane, simply select the page you want to view at the top and choose View⇨View as Root (Windows) or Site⇨Site Map View⇨ View as Root (Macintosh) from the Menu bar.

 Adjust the spacing between columns by clicking the arrow at the end of any connecting line and dragging it to change the length of the line.

Combination Site Files/Site Map View

 To view your site with site files in one pane and a Site Map in another pane, switch to the Site window. Click and hold down the Site Map View button and choose Map and Files from the pop-up menu. Alternatively, you can choose Window⇨Site Map from the Menu bar.

Press to expand view   Design Notes attached to this page

Site Map pane   Site Files pane

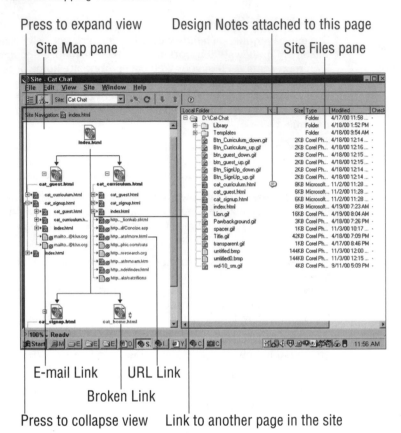

E-mail Link   URL Link

Broken Link

Press to collapse view   Link to another page in the site

Your Site Map appears in the left pane of your Site window, and your site files appear in the right pane. Adjust the size of either pane by dragging its window frame.

Part XIII

Streamlining Your Work

If you choose to build 20-page — or 200-page — Web sites, you may want to invoke as many timesaving tactics as Dreamweaver offers. From setting default preferences (such as text formatting and layer size) to creating reusable document templates, you can take advantage of Dreamweaver's extensive customization options to help streamline your work. Dreamweaver even offers a History panel that records your page-building actions as you work — and lets you undo or repeat an entire group of actions as you choose.

To help you keep track of all your dependent files, Dreamweaver 4 provides a new Assets panel where you can log such objects as images, Flash movies, and scripts you use in constructing your pages. You can also store assets that you use repeatedly throughout your site in the Dreamweaver Library. Any change to an asset can be made once in the Library and then applied automatically to every instance of the asset throughout your site.

In this part . . .

Assembling Assets

 Assets are dependent files that are Web objects accessed by your HTML pages. The Assets panel is a one-stop location for examining all the assets of a particular Web site. Assets are listed by their name, size, type, and full path. You can open the Assets panel by choosing Window⇨Assets from the Menu bar or by clicking the Assets button on either the Launcher or Mini-Launcher.

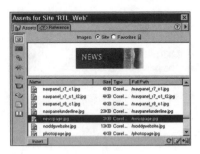

Assets are categorized by type and include images, colors, URLs, Flash files, Shockwave files, movies, scripts, templates, and Library objects. You can view all assets of a particular type by clicking the associated button in the Assets panel.

Managing site assets

You can perform the following management tasks on your assets:

- ✔ **Access Asset Favorites:** Click the Favorites radio button in the Assets panel.

- ✔ **Add an asset to the Assets panel:** Create and save an asset in a folder contained in your site root.

- ✔ **Add an asset to your Favorites list:** For any site, select an asset in the Assets panel and click the Add to Favorites button.

- ✔ **Delete an asset:** Delete the asset in your site files or in the Assets panel.

- ✔ **Edit an asset:** Select the asset in the Assets panel and click the Edit button. An editing program for the asset file type opens your selection. Edit your asset and save your work.

- ✔ **Refresh the asset list:** Click the Refresh button.

- ✔ **View assets:** Click an asset type button in the Assets panel. All available assets for the current site are listed.

Checking out Library assets

The Dreamweaver Library is comprised of objects that make up a special asset group of their own. A *Library asset* is an object that you can edit in the Dreamweaver Library; every occurrence of that asset is automatically updated throughout your site. Save yourself time by creating a Library asset for an object that you use repeatedly throughout your site, such as a logo. You can perform the following tasks using the Dreamweaver Library:

✔ **Add a new Library asset:** Click the Library button at the Assets panel and then click the New Library Item button at the bottom of the panel. A new, untitled Library asset is created. You can enter a name for the asset while it is selected.

✔ **Delete a Library asset:** Select the asset in the Library category of the Assets panel and click Delete.

✔ **Edit a Library asset:** Select the asset in the Library category of the Assets panel and click the Edit button. An editing program for the asset file type opens your selection. Edit your asset and save your work.

✔ **Insert a Library asset into a document:** Position your mouse cursor where you want to add the asset. Then select the asset you want to use and click the Insert button on the Assets panel.

✔ **Move an existing asset to the Library:** Click and drag the asset from the Document window into the Library category of the Assets panel. An untitled copy of the new asset is created. Enter a name for the asset while it is selected.

Library assets use . l i b as their filename extension

Keyboard Shortcuts

As you become proficient at using Dreamweaver, you can use keyboard shortcuts to expedite tasks you otherwise perform using panels on the Menu bar. Memorizing and using keyboard shortcuts is especially useful for actions you perform repeatedly, such as inserting a named anchor (Ctrl+Alt+A in Windows) when updating a daily news page and its companion table of contents. You can access a complete list of keyboard shortcuts by choosing Help⇨ Using Dreamweaver from the Menu bar. Switch to the Index and then scroll down the index and click Keyboard Shortcuts.

The following table lists some of the more commonly used Windows and Macintosh keyboard shortcuts.

Windows Keys	*Mac Keys*	*Action*
Ctrl+Home	Cmd+Home	Top of Current Cell
Ctrl+End	Cmd+End	Bottom of Current Cell
Ctrl+spacebar	Cmd+spacebar	Update Table
Ctrl+tab	Cmd+tab	Switch View, Switch Window
Ctrl+A	Cmd+A	Select All
Ctrl+B	Cmd+B	Bold
Ctrl+C	Cmd+C	Copy
Ctrl+E	Cmd+E	Edit with External Editor
Ctrl+F	Cmd+F	Find and Replace
Ctrl+I	Cmd+I	Italic
Ctrl+J	Cmd+J	Page Properties
Ctrl+L	Cmd+L	Make/Change Link
Ctrl+N	Cmd+N	New; New File
Ctrl+O	Cmd+O	Open, Remove Formatting
Ctrl+Q	Cmd+Q	Quit
Ctrl+S	Cmd+S	Save, Update
Ctrl+T	Cmd+T	Paragraph Format, Quick Tag Editor
Ctrl+U	Cmd+U	Preferences
Ctrl+V	Cmd+V	Paste
Ctrl+W	Cmd+W	Close
Ctrl+X	Cmd+X	Cut
Ctrl+Y	Cmd+Y	Redo
Ctrl+Z	Cmd+Z	Undo
Ctrl+F1	Cmd+F1	Help — Dreamweaver Support Center
Ctrl+F2	Cmd+F2	Object Panel
Ctrl+F3	Cmd+F3	Property Inspector
Ctrl+F6	Cmd+F6	Layout View
Ctrl+F8	Cmd+F8	Check Links Sitewide
Ctrl+F11	Cmd+F1	CSS Styles

Windows Keys	Mac Keys	Action
Ctrl+Alt+]	Cmd+Opt+]	Indent
Ctrl+Alt+[	Cmd+Opt+[	Outdent
Ctrl+Alt+A	Cmd+Opt+A	Named Anchors
Ctrl+Alt+F	Cmd+Opt+F	Flash Movie
Ctrl+Alt+G	Cmd+Opt+G	Snap to Grid
Ctrl+Alt+I	Cmd+Opt+I	Insert Image
Ctrl+Alt+S	Cmd+Opt+S	Split Cell
Ctrl+Alt+T	Cmd+Opt+T	Insert Table
Ctrl+Shift+C	Cmd+Shift+C	Copy HTML
Ctrl+Shift+L	Cmd+Shift+L	Remove Link
Ctrl+Shift+S	Cmd+Shift+S	Save As
Ctrl+Shift+V	Cmd+Shift+V	Paste HTML
Ctrl+Shift+W	Cmd+Shift+W	Head Content
Ctrl+Shift+X	Cmd+Shift+X	Start/Stop Recording Command
Ctrl+Shift+Spacebar	Cmd+Shift+Spacebar	Non-breaking space
F1	F1	Help — Using Dreamweaver
F2	F2	Layers
F3	F3	Find Next
F4	F4	Show/Hide Panels
F8	F8	Site Files
F10	F10	HTML Code Inspector
F11	F11	Assets
Shift+Enter	Shift+Return	Link Break
Shift+F1	Shift+F1	Reference
Shift+F2	Shift+F2	Frames
Shift+F3	Shift+F3	Behaviors
Shift+F4	Shift+F4	Minimize All
Shift+F7	Shift+F7	Check Spelling
Shift+F8	Cmd+F8	Check Links Sitewide
Shift+F9	Shift+F9	Timelines Inspector
Shift+F10	Shift+F10	History

You can edit existing keyboard shortcuts and create new ones of your own at the Keyboard Shortcuts dialog box. Open it by choosing Edit⇔Keyboard Shortcuts from the Menu bar.

Recording History

The History panel records all recent actions performed on your document. The default number of actions recorded is 50, but you can change this number in the General category of Dreamweaver Preferences. (*See also* "Setting Preferences" in this part.)

 Open the History panel by clicking the History button in the Launcher or Mini-Launcher or by choosing Window⇔History from the Menu bar.

You can perform the following actions in the History panel:

- ✔ **Undo actions:** Drag the slider arrow up to the last action that you want maintained. All actions following your selected action are undone.

- ✔ **Replay actions:** Select an action in the History panel and click the Replay button to repeat that action. Designate a sequence of actions for replay by holding down the Shift key as you select the actions. Action icons that include a red *X* cannot be replayed.

- ✔ **Save selected steps as a command:** Select the steps you want to save and then click the Disk button in the History panel. At the Save As Command dialog box, enter a Command Name and click OK. Saving a series of steps as a command can expedite tasks you perform repeatedly. For example, you may perform an image formatting procedure that consists of resizing the dimensions of an image and adding a border of a certain color and width to the image. You can instead replace this series of steps with a single command.

Setting Preferences

Dreamweaver Preferences enable you to customize almost all aspects of your work activity in the Dreamweaver program. The Preferences dialog box is where you set up default settings for the options you select most frequently while working.

Open the Preferences dialog box by choosing Edit⇨Preferences from the Menu bar.

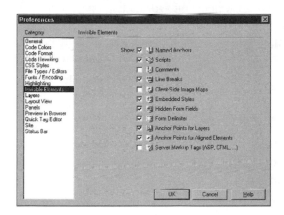

At the Preferences dialog box, set your personal choices for the following categories:

- ✔ **General:** Set file and editing options, including default file naming.

- ✔ **Code Colors:** Set background and text colors for viewing HTML source code.

- ✔ **Code Format:** Set HTML source code formatting, including indents and line breaks.

- ✔ **Code Rewriting:** Set rewrite conditions for fixing erroneously formatted HTML source code.

- ✔ **CSS Styles:** Set conditions for using shorthand when creating and editing CSS Styles. CSS Styles enable you to create custom formatting for text and other page features. You can save the formatting as a style that you can apply throughout your site. An advantage of using CSS text is that users cannot change the appearance of your text in their browsers, thus retaining your intended layout regardless of their browser preferences.

✔ **File Types/Editors:** Set file types for opening in code view as well as external editors.

✔ **Fonts/Encoding:** Set default font and formatting for page text, along with language encoding.

✔ **Highlighting:** Select color for highlighting editable and locked regions, plus library items and third-party tags.

✔ **Invisible Elements:** Identify the invisibles (including named anchors and layers) that you want to show while editing.

✔ **Layers:** Specify default layer attributes, including size and visibility.

✔ **Layout View:** Set layout view colors and spacer image attributes. Spacer images are used in conjunction with the Autostretch feature when laying out tables.

✔ **Panels:** Specify which panels and inspectors you want to show on top and in the launcher.

✔ **Preview in Browser:** Set your preview browsers, including the primary browser for preview.

✔ **Quick Tag Editor:** Set delay time for updating code and enable or disable tag hints.

✔ **Site:** Set Site Files view and FTP connection properties.

✔ **Status Bar:** Set window size dimensions and descriptions, connection speed, and launcher visibility.

Using Page Templates

If multiple pages in your Web site use the same basic design and information, you can construct them from a template. A *template* is a page that consists of both *editable regions* and *locked regions* that you can assemble based on which regions of your page change and which regions stay the same. When you create Web pages from your unique template, you can customize the editable regions on each page, while leaving the locked regions to appear identically from page to page.

Creating a template

To create a new template, follow this procedure:

1. Create a new blank document by choosing File⇨New from the Menu bar.

   Alternatively, you can create a template from an existing document by choosing File⇨Open from the Menu bar or by double-clicking the document filename from the Site Files window.

2. Choose File⇨Save as Template from the Menu bar.

3. In the Save As Template dialog box, enter a name for the template in the Save As box.

4. Edit the document to create the template design you want.

   Some regions of your layout are meant to stay locked while others are set as editable. You don't have to define whether a region is locked or editable in this step; simply create regions to hold the template's content. For example, create a layer where you can place a logo or masthead, and create another layer where you can place text.

5. To create an editable region, select the object you want to affect and choose Modify⇨Templates⇨New Editable Region from the Menu bar.

   You can mark as editable a layer, a layer's contents, a table cell, or an entire table. Regions that you do not create as editable remain locked automatically.

6. In the New Editable Region dialog box, enter a name for the region at the Name box.

7. Click OK to close the dialog box. The new editable region is created and labeled on your template.

8. Repeat Steps 5 through 7 to create as many editable regions as you want.

9. Choose File⇨Save from the Menu bar.

Remove an existing editable region by clicking the region and choosing Modify⇨Templates⇨New Editable Region from the Menu bar. Select the name of the region you want to lock and click OK.

Applying a template

Create a new document using a template by choosing File⇨New from Template. The new document shows the name of its base template in the Document window and displays all editable regions in highlighted boundaries. Make your edits in the editable regions and save the document with a .htm or .html file extension.

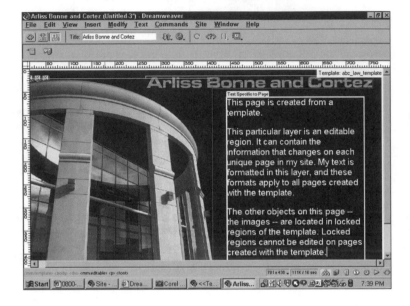

Part XIV

Publishing and Updating Your Site

To make your Web site available online, you must sign up with a hosting service — or have some other method of accessing a server on the Word Wide Web. You can then transfer a copy of your entire local site root to a folder on the Web server that hosts your site. You must transfer not only every HTML code page in your local site but also every image, video, and sound (and all other files you use in your site) to the remote host.

After your site is transferred, you and other collaborators can retrieve site pages, work on them locally, and then upload the pages back to the host to keep the site updated. You can also check and change links sitewide quickly and easily to ensure that users don't access any dead-end pages from your site.

In this part . . .

Collaborating on Site Revisions

Site maintenance can be an enormous task that you can accomplish best by giving multiple designers revision privileges for files on the site host. To simplify the maintenance task, Dreamweaver provides a Check In/Check Out system that enables you to work collaboratively with others in revising site files. This system helps you and your team keep track of who has which file currently checked out — so that revisers don't inadvertently duplicate editing efforts.

Enabling file Check In/Check Out

You can set up file check in/out for a site as follows:

1. In Dreamweaver, choose S̲ite⇨De̲fine Sites from the Menu bar to open the Define Site dialog box.

2. From the Site list, select the site that you want to work on and click the E̲dit button. Doing so opens the Site Definition dialog box for your site.

3. Select the Remote Info category.

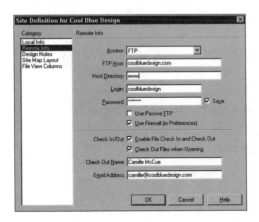

4. If you select FTP or Local/Network for your Access method, click the E̲nable File Check In and Check Out check box. If you select SourceSafe Database or WebDAV for your Access method, click the Settings button and complete the dialog box that appears.

5. For all Access methods, click the C̲heck Out Files when Opening check box. Doing so automatically marks a file as checked out to you whenever you open it from the remote server.

6. If you selected FTP or Local/Network for your Access method, enter a Check Out Name and E-Mail Address. Any file you check out will show this name and address listed in the Check Out column of the Remote Files pane of the Site window.

Checking files in and out

Follow these procedures to check files in and out for collaborative site editing:

 To check files out: In the Remote Files pane of the Site window, select the files you want to check out. Then click the Check Out button at the top of the Site window or choose Site⇒Check Out from the Menu bar. The Checked Out By column in the remote pane of the Site window identifies the person checking out the file. A check mark appears in front of the filename to indicate that it is checked out.

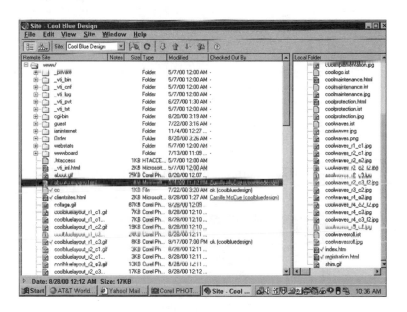

 To check files in: In the remote pane, select the files you want to check in. Then click the Check In button at the top of the Site window or choose Site⇒Check In from the Menu bar. The Checked Out By column in the remote pane of the Site window removes the name of the person who had previously checked out the file. Also, the check mark in front of the filename indicating its checked out status is removed.

Connecting to a Web Server

 To connect to your Web Server, simply click the Connect to Remote Host button in the Site window. Alternatively, you can choose Site⇨ Connect from the Menu bar. After you connect, your site files on the remote host appear in the *Remote Files pane* — the left pane of the Site window. Files of your local site root still show in the right pane of the Site window.

 When you are done working with your Web server, simply click the Disconnect from Remote Host button in the Site window. Alternatively, you can choose Site⇨Disconnect from the Menu bar.

Defining Remote Host Settings

Dreamweaver makes an easy task of transferring Web files from your local site to the remote host. But prior to transferring, or *uploading,* your first site to the host, you must tell Dreamweaver some basic information about the host, such as where it is located on the Web and what the access password is.

You define remote host attributes in the same dialog box that you use to define your local site — namely the Site Definition dialog box. Follow these steps:

1. In Dreamweaver, choose Site⇨Define Sites from the Menu bar to open the Define Sites dialog box.

2. From the Site list, select the site you want to work on and click the Edit button. Doing so opens the Site Definition dialog box for your site.

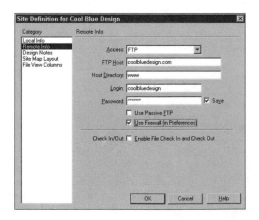

3. Select the Remote Info category.

4. At the Access drop-down menu, select a Web server access method from these options:

None: Applicable only if you do not plan to upload your site to a remove server.

FTP: Select this option to transfer files to and from your server via File Transfer Protocol. Supply the requested information at the dialog box:

Item	*Description*
FTP Host	Enter the name of the FTP connection for your server, such as www.domainname.com
Host Directory	Enter the name from which users will access your site, such as www or www/public/mccue
Login	Enter your login identification for accessing the server
Password	Enter your password for accessing the server and click the Save check box if you want Dreamweaver to remember your password
Use Passive FTP check box	Check this box if your firewall requires that your local software establish the server connection instead of the remote host
Use Firewall check box	Check this box if you connect to the host from behind a firewall

Local/Network: Select this option if your local computer is also your Web server or if you connect to the Web server via a local area network. At the Remote Folder box, enter a folder name or browse to select the folder on the remote host where you store your site files. Click to check the Refresh Remote File List Automatically box if you want to see the Remote Files pane of the Site window updated automatically as you transfer files to the remote server.

SourceSafeDatabase: Select this option if you want to access a SourceSafe database. Click the Settings button and complete the Open SourceSafe Database dialog box by typing (or browsing for) a Database Path, typing a Project Name, and providing your username and password.

WebDAV: Select this option if you want to make a WebDAV connection. Click the Settings button and complete the WebDAV Connection dialog box by entering the server URL and providing your username, password, and e-mail address.

5. Click OK to close the Site Definition dialog box.

6. Click Done to close the Define Sites dialog box.

Are you confused about information regarding your Web server? Contact your hosting service or your system administrator to find out the server name, directory, username, password, and other details you need to complete the Remote Info area of the Site Definition dialog box.

If you change hosting services or other remote server information, such as your password, you can edit your Remote Host attributes by returning to the Site Definition dialog box.

Measuring Download Time

Download time is an important measurement for you as a Web designer because it tells you how long users must wait to view your entire page on their computers. Download time depends on the connection speed, or *baud rate,* of a user's modem.

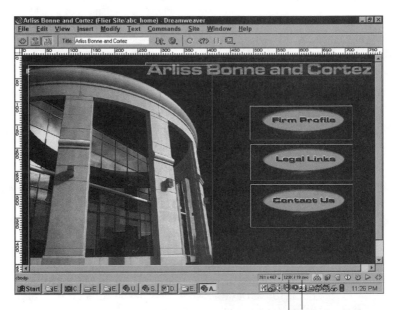

Download time

File size

You can keep tabs on the expected download time for a page under construction by looking at the File Size/Download Time indicator in the Status Bar at the bottom of the Document window.

To enable Dreamweaver to compute the expected download time, you must set an expected user connection speed in Dreamweaver Preferences. Simply choose Edit⇔Preferences from the Menu bar to open the Preferences dialog box. At the Preferences dialog box, select the Status Bar category and then select a connection speed at the Connection Speed drop-down menu. Choices consist of 14.4, 28.8, 33.6, 56, 64, 128, or 1500 Kilobits per second.

Try minimizing download time for a page to the greatest degree possible prior to uploading it to the server. Then check the actual download time after the page goes online to determine whether additional file size reduction is needed.

Monitoring Links on the Web

After constructing your site and putting it on the Web, you can monitor its currency by frequently checking that any absolute address links you set up still work as intended. URLs change frequently, and you don't want users to click on links that don't open their intended destinations. (*See also* Part XII for details on checking external links.)

Setting your HTTP address

To assist Dreamweaver in checking link accuracy, you can provide the actual URL for your site on the Web. Dreamweaver uses this information to check whether links in your site refer to other pages in your site root or to absolute addresses external to your site. Set your HTTP address as follows:

1. In Dreamweaver, choose Site⇔Define Sites from the Menu bar to open the Define Sites dialog box.

2. From the Site list, select the site you want to work on and click the Edit button. Doing so opens the Site Definition dialog box for your site.

3. Select the Local Info category.

4. At the HTTP Address box, enter the URL for your site. This URL is the actual Web address for your site, for instance, http://www.yoursite.com.

5. Click OK to close the Site Definition dialog box.

6. Click Done to close the Define Sites dialog box.

Click to check the Enable Cache check box in the Local Info category of the Site Definition dialog box. Enabling cache causes file and assets information to be maintained in the site. This helps speed up site management tasks as you construct your site. You can rebuild the cache at any time by choosing Site⇔Recreate Site Cache from the Menu bar.

Updating links sitewide

The Dreamweaver Link Checker can tell you whether links in your site are functioning properly (*see also* Part XII). If you do find an incorrect link, you can update the link throughout your site, whether it's a URL or a link to one of your own pages. Just follow this procedure:

1. Choose Site⇔Change Link Sitewide from the Menu bar.

   Doing so opens the Change Link dialog box where you can replace the name of an old link with its new name.

2. In the Change All Links To box, enter the current URL or internal page name or address you want to change.

3. In the Into Links To box, enter the URL or internal page of what you want the links to change to.

4. Click OK.

Dreamweaver changes your links sitewide and updates the HTML page code for all the affected pages.

Setting Up <meta> Tags

Your goal in putting a Web site online is probably to make a certain body of information accessible to the public. Search engines can help users track down your site, but you can improve the likelihood that search engines list your site by including special HTML code on your pages. This special code is contained in <meta> tags and consists of keywords and descriptions that you create to help search engines match user queries with pages comprising your site.

Adding keyword <meta> tags

Set up keyword <meta> tags for a page as follows:

1. In the Document window, click the Insert Keyword button from the Head Objects panel. Alternatively, you can choose Insert⇨ Head Tags⇨Keywords from the Menu bar.

2. In the Insert Keywords dialog box, enter individual words or phrases that describe the content of your page. Separate entries with commas.

Search engines use these keywords to index the page.

3. Click OK. Doing so closes the dialog box and inserts your entries into the <meta> keyword tag in the HTML page code.

Adding a description <meta> tag

Set up a description <meta> tag for a page as follows:

1. In the Document window, click the Insert Description button from the Head Objects panel. Alternatively, you can choose Insert⇨Head Tags⇨Description from the Menu bar.

2. At the Insert Description dialog box, enter a sentence or paragraph that describes the content of your page. Search engines use this description to index the page.

3. Click OK. Doing so closes the dialog box and inserts your entry into the <meta> description tag and the HTML page code.

Add <meta> tags to a page template and then use the template to construct pages in your site. Every page you create with the template automatically possesses the <meta> tags you set up.

Transferring Files

As soon as you connect to the remote host, you can transfer files to and from the server. Just follow these steps:

1. If you're not already at the Site window, switch to it by choosing Window⇨Site Files from the Menu bar.

2. Select the files you want to transfer.

   To select files you want to send to the remote site: Click on one or more files in the Local Files pane.

   To select files you want to retrieve from the remote site: Click on one or more files in the Remote Files pane.

3. Transfer the files.

   To send local files to the remote site: Click the Put button in the Site window or choose Site⇨Put from the Menu bar. Dreamweaver presents a dialog box that asks whether you want to include dependent files in the transfer. Dependent files are files, such as images, that are called by your HTML code pages. Click Yes to include these files or No to transfer only your selected files.

   To bring remote files to the local site: Click the Get button in the Site window or choose Site⇨Get from the Menu bar.

Your transferred files appear in the destination window pane. You can move files in and out of folders in their new location using standard Windows procedures.

At any time, you can refresh your file lists to re-read a directory of files. To refresh the selected file directory, just click the Refresh button in the Site window.

Halt a file transfer in progress by clicking the Stop Current Task button in the Site window.

Glossary: Tech Talk

absolute address: A URL (Uniform Resource Locator) on the Web.

action: In a behavior, the activity that is executed as a result of an event.

alternative text: Text that is displayed in place of an image. Many Internet users speed their Web surfing activities by disabling automatic downloading of images, choosing instead to view an image only if the alternative text description catches their interest.

Animation bar: A bar you add to a channel on a Timeline that defines the animation of a single object over a period of time.

assets: Dependent files that are Web objects accessed by your HTML pages. Assets are categorized as images, colors, URLs, Flash files, Shockwave files, movies, scripts, templates, or Library objects.

autostretch: An option that enables you to make a table stretch to fill the entire width of a user's browser. Only one column in a table can be set to autostretch.

behavior: A JavaScript action that is executed in a Web browser when the user performs some sort of event. Many behaviors serve a navigational function in the Web site.

Cascading Style Sheets (CSS) Style: A style you set up that enables you to format your pages in such a way that users' browsers cannot modify your exact specifications. You can modify text formatting, fonts, sizes, colors, and styles — as well as numerous other page attributes, including positioning and backgrounds.

check box: A form object that a user can click to select and click again to deselect the item. Presenting multiple check boxes enables the user to select as many of the items listed as applicable.

design notes: Comments that you and others working on a Web site can attach to site pages for the purpose of documenting page status.

dialog box: A box that appears when you must enter additional information about a page object or action. Dialog boxes do not stay open while you work — they vanish after you enter and submit the needed information or press the Cancel button.

document-relative address: An address that identifies where the link file is located relative to the current document.

Document window: Your primary workspace in Dreamweaver 4. The Document window provides you with a graphical environment to construct your individual Web pages. You can view the Document window full screen or you can choose the Split View where you can view the Document window and the HTML source code for your page at the same time.

download time: A measurement that tells you how long users must wait to view your entire page on their computers.

drop-down menu: A form object that presents a list of choices from which the user can make a selection. Only one choice shows on-screen until the user clicks the drop-down arrow to see the other choices. The user can select only a single item from the list of choices. When the user makes a choice, that selection becomes the item that shows on-screen.

E-mail link: A link that opens a new e-mail message window when a user clicks it. The new message window contains the user's e-mail address in the From box and the e-mail address you specify in the To box.

event: What a user does in order to execute a behavior on a Web page.

Flash button: A button that plays a miniature Flash movie when the user rolls the mouse pointer over it. You can create the Flash button directly in Dreamweaver.

Flash text: Text that changes colors when the user rolls the mouse pointer over it. The text object is a Flash movie that you can create directly in Dreamweaver.

form: An object that provides users with a structured region for entering specific information that can be gathered and transmitted back to the host computer.

frames: Divisions of a Web page that enable you to independently load information into distinct regions of your page.

frameset: A special HTML page that defines the structure and formatting of frames on your Web page.

Get: The process of transferring files from the host to your local computer.

grid: Graph paper for the Document window. The grid consists of equally spaced horizontal and vertical lines that can visually assist you in positioning and aligning page elements.

History panel: A panel that records your page-building actions as you work and lets you undo or repeat an entire group of actions as you choose.

horizontal rule: A line image that creates a visual break between content on a Web page.

hotspot: An active area of an image that a user can click to open a link to another Web page or activate a behavior. Hotspots can be shaped like rectangles, circles, or polygons (irregular objects).

HTML (Hypertext Markup Language): The computer language used to set up and display pages for viewing on the Web. Dreamweaver translates your work into HTML code for each Web page you create.

HTML style: A text style you set up that enables you to use a single, aggregate step to replace multiple individual steps in creating text attributes.

image maps: Images with hot spot regions.

image padding: Vertical or horizontal standoff space between the image and any elements surrounding it.

invisible elements: Yellow markers in the Document window that represent page objects, such as layers and named anchors.

Jump menu: A form object that provides users with a list of pages to jump to on your site.

keyframe: In timeline animation, a frame that establishes a starting point from which subsequent construction progresses. A timeline can possess multiple keyframes spread throughout its sequence of frames. Each keyframe contains details about a particular stage of an object in an animation.

layer: A rectangular holding region of the Document window. You can create a layer of any size and position it anywhere in the window. You can put anything you want — text, graphics, forms, videos — inside a layer. You can also overlap or stack layers.

layer overflow: How objects in a layer are displayed if the objects exceed the layer boundaries. For example, you can include a scroll bar so that users can scroll to view text that extends beyond the boundary of the layer.

Layout View: A view specifically geared toward helping you design your Web pages using tables. The advantage of the Layout View is that it provides special tools for drawing and editing tables and table cells.

link: An object that a user clicks in order to navigate to another location. Links are most frequently created from text and images.

local site root: The set of files on your computer that you create and assemble to build a Web site.

low source image: A simplified version of a large file size image that you include on a Web page. The low source image has a smaller file size and faster download time than the main image.

line break: A break that causes your cursor to move to the start of the next line, without creating a paragraph break.

link: A connection to another location on the current page, to another Web page in the current site, or to a URL on the Web. Links enable you to direct visitors to related content located away from the current object.

<meta> tags: HTML code placed at the beginning of your Web page and consisting of keywords and descriptions that you create to help search engines match user queries with your page.

named anchor: A navigational link that connects users not just to a Web page but also to a specific location on the page.

Navigation bar: A group of buttons that users can access to move throughout your Web site. Buttons within a Navigation bar may present users with such options as moving backwards, moving forwards, returning to the home page, or jumping to specific pages within the site.

nested layer: A layer that has a dependent relationship with another layer. The nested layer is often referred to as the *child* layer, and the layer on which it depends is called the *parent* layer.

Quick Tag Editor: Shows the HTML code for the currently selected page object. Press the Quick Tag Editor icon in the Property inspector for the selected object to open the Quick Tag Editor.

page properties: Controls the look of several key page attributes, including the title of the page, page background color, link colors, and page margins.

panel: A Dreamweaver tool area that lets you work on a particular set of page features. For example, the Layers panel lists information about all the layers on the current page, and also enables you to edit certain attributes of those layers. The Objects panel lets you add such features as images, tables, and media to your pages without accessing menus.

Preferences: Settings that enable you to customize almost all aspects of your work activity in the Dreamweaver program. The Preferences dialog box is where you set up default settings for the options that you select most frequently while working.

Property inspector: A Dreamweaver tool area that lets you work on numerous attributes of a single page object, such as a selection of text or an image. For example, selecting text on a page opens the Text Property inspector, where you can format the text size, font, color, link, and other information.

Put: The process of transferring files from your local computer to the host.

Radio buttons: Form objects that present the user with a list of items from which only a single item can be selected.

Reference panel: Offers a dictionary-style reference on CSS, HTML, and JavaScript.

rollover image: An image that appears to change when the user rolls the mouse pointer over it. Rollovers add interactivity to a Web page by helping users know what parts of the page link to other Web pages.

rulers: Available at the top and left sides of the Document window to help you measure and numerically position page elements.

scrolling list: A form object that presents a list of choices from which the form user can make a selection. You can include as many choices as you want in the menu, and you can choose how many items appear on-screen in the list, an attribute called the *list height*

Site Files View: A view in which you see a list of all the HTML documents and dependent files contained in your site, grouped by folder.

Site Map View: A view in which you see your site graphically. A document icon represents each of your Web pages, with lines connecting the document icons to show the relationship between Web pages in the site.

site root-relative address: An address that indicates where the link file is located relative to the primary directory of the current site.

Site window: A window where you can examine your entire site. You can view a list of all files in your site and a map of how those files connect together. The Site window is also where you connect to the host server so that you can transfer your site from your local computer to the Web.

spacer image: A placeholder that is added to the column that you designate for stretching when using the autostretch feature. The spacer image is a transparent image that cannot be seen in the browser.

Standard View: The WYSIWYG (what-you-see-is-what-you-get) view in which you lay out pages in the Document window.

streaming media: Audio and video files that can begin playing as soon as sufficient information has been transferred to the user's computer to stay ahead of the remaining portion of the file as it downloads. Streaming enables the user to experience your clip much sooner than with a downloadable file.

table: A page object that consists of holding areas (or *cells*) where you can place virtually any Web element, such as text or an image. Cells are organized horizontally into *rows* and vertically into *columns*.

target: The frame where linked content is presented.

template: A specially formatted Web page that you can use to construct multiple pages in your Web site that use the same basic design. A *template* consists of both *editable regions* and *locked regions* that you can assemble based on which regions of your pages change and which regions stay the same.

timeline: Creating animation in Dreamweaver hinges on manipulating the timeline. You use the timeline to define which page objects show, how they are positioned, and what other media are playing any time a user is viewing your Web page. The timeline enables you to change all these items from one second to the next, creating a motion-enriched page.

tracing image: An image you can import from a graphics program and use as a blueprint for designing a page.

visibility: A layer attribute that defines whether the layer shows or is hidden. You can cause the visibility of a layer to change based on user actions.

Window Size indicator: Shows the resolution of the target monitor you are building your Web site for display in. The higher the resolution, the larger the workspace in your Document window.

z-index: Indicates the position of a layer in a stack of multiple layers. Z-indexes are measured in whole numbers. Layers with larger z-indexes obscure those with smaller z-indexes.

Index